The Craft
of
Novel-Writing

Dianne Doubtfire

The Craft
of
Novel-Writing

A practical guide

Allison & Busby
London and New York

First published
in Great Britain 1978 by
Allison & Busby Limited,
6a Noel Street, London W1V 3RB
Reprinted 1979

This revised edition first published 1981 by
Allison & Busby Limited and distributed in the USA by
Schocken Books Inc.,
200 Madison Avenue, New York, NY 10016

British Library Cataloguing in Publication Data:
D. Doubtfire, Dianne
    The craft of novel-writing—New rev. ed.
    1. Fiction—Authorship
    I. Title
    808.33   PN3355
ISBN   0-85031-405-4-pbk

Set in Times
by Malvern Typesetting Services Ltd
and printed in Great Britain by
Biddles Ltd, Guildford, Surrey

Contents

Acknowledgements

The author and publishers are grateful to the following authors, publishers, agents and literary executors for permission to include copyright material:

Nigel Balchin, *The Small Back Room*; David Higham Associates and William Collins Sons & Co. Ltd.; Lynne Reid Banks, *The L-Shaped Room*: Lynne Reid Banks, Chatto & Windus Ltd., Simon & Schuster Inc. and Bolt & Watson Ltd.; Stan Barstow, *A Raging Calm*: Stan Barstow and John Farquharson Ltd.; H. E. Bates, *Love for Lydia*: the estate of the late H. E. Bates, Michael Joseph Ltd. and Laurence Pollinger Ltd.; Saul Bellow, *Herzog*: Saul Bellow and Weidenfeld & Nicolson Ltd.; Elizabeth Bowen, *The Death of the Heart*: the estate of Elizabeth Bowen and Alfred A. Knopf Inc.; John Braine, *Room at the Top*: John Braine, Eyre & Spottiswoode Ltd. and David Higham Associates; Albert Camus, *The Outsider* (published abroad as *The Stranger*): copyright © 1942 by Albert Camus, translation by Stuart Gilbert copyright © 1946 by Hamish Hamilton Ltd., London; *Carnets 1942–1951* (published abroad as *Notebooks 1942–1951*): copyright © 1964 by Editions Gallimard, translation by Philip Thody copyright © 1966 by Hamish Hamilton Ltd., London: Alfred A. Knopf Inc.; Joyce Cary, *A Fearful Joy*: the estate of Joyce Cary and Curtis Brown Ltd.; Ivy Compton-Burnett, Conversation with M. Jourdain (*Orion*, 1945): Victor Gollancz Ltd; Feodor Dostoevsky, *Letters*, translated by Ethel Colburn Mayne: Chatto & Windus Ltd.; Margaret Drabble, *The Realms of Gold*: Margaret Drabble and A. D. Peters & Co. Ltd.; Nell Dunn, *Poor Cow*: Nell Dunn, MacGibbon & Kee Ltd/Granada Publishing Ltd.; Laurence Durrell, *Balthazar*: Laurence Durrell and E. P. Dutton; E. M. Forster, *Aspects of the Novel*: Edward Arnold (Publishers) Ltd.; Pamela Frankau, *Pen to Paper*: William Heinemann Ltd. and A. P. Watt Ltd.; A. B. Goldenweizer, *Talks with Tolstoi*: Hogarth Press/Chatto & Windus Ltd.; Robert Graves, television interview: Robert Graves and A. P. Watt Ltd.; Graham Greene, *A Burnt-Out Case*: copyright © 1961 by Graham Greene, reprinted by permission of Viking Penguin Inc.; Graham Greene, *Travels with my Aunt*: copyright © 1969 by Graham Greene, reprinted by permission of Viking Penguin Inc.; John Masters, *Bhowani Junction*: copyright © 1954 by John Masters, reprinted by permission of Viking Penguin Inc.; François Mauriac, *God and Mammon*: Sheed & Ward Ltd.; Alberto Moravia, *Man as an End*, translated by Bernard Wall: copyright © Martin Secker & Warburg Ltd., 1966: Farrar, Straus & Giroux Inc.; Penelope Mortimer, *The Pumpkin Eater*: Penelope Mortimer and A. D. Peters & Co. Ltd.; Iris Murdoch, *The Sacred and Profane Love Machine*: copyright © 1974 by Iris Murdoch, and *Under the Net*,

The author would also like to express her deep gratitude to all those personal friends who read the book in typescript and helped her to improve it. And to her husband, Stanley, for his unfailing support and encouragement.

With love and gratitude
to all my Swanwick friends

Foreword

Other than winning the Pools or the Lottery, the easiest way of making a fortune is to write a novel. After all, everyone has a book in him or her and it takes little effort to set it down on paper.

Those are beliefs which are widely held, but which are quite untrue. Few novels make fortunes for their authors, and the books which are in everybody should usually stay there; but the principal fallacy is the suggestion that writing a novel is easy. As the title of this book rightly proclaims, novel-writing is a craft, and no craft, particularly one as specialised as this, is easy or can be practised successfully without first learning how it is done.

Because the creation of a work of fiction is a highly individual enterprise, Dianne Doubtfire has wisely avoided making her advice too specific – genius rarely adheres strictly to the rules. But for those novelists who are not in the genius class, and especially for beginners, she has provided an invaluable guide to the basics of the craft.

Brief though it is, *The Craft of Novel-Writing* packs in a vast amount of practical help, presented with a fine simplicity. Not the least of its values is its revelation of Dianne Doubtfire's love of her subject and her willingness, like any good teacher, to share that love with her readers. Follow her precepts, avoid the pitfalls which she points out, perhaps on occasion disagree with her (for thoughtful disagreement may itself prove to be a teaching aid), and you cannot help but improve your writing.

I very much welcome this excellent book.

Michael Legat
(Formerly Editorial Director of Corgi Books
and, more recently, of Cassell)

Introduction

Writing a successful novel demands not only talent and determination but also a high degree of craftsmanship. No textbook can supply talent or determination, but craftsmanship is another matter.

It is twenty-five years since I began, through trial and error, to learn the techniques of novel-writing, and I hope this practical guide-book will help the novice to acquire the necessary skills more speedily than I did. It deals simply and directly with the nuts and bolts of the craft, and is intended mainly for those who are embarking on their first book. Nevertheless, I hope there may be something of interest to the practising novelist, too; most of us enjoy reading about the mechanics of writing.

I shall be dealing with the so-called "straight" novel – not the historical, romantic, detective and experimental kind – but much of the information in the following chapters can be applied to any full-length work of fiction. I think the potential novelist is well advised to study the accepted techniques, even though he or she may eventually be brave and brilliant enough to ignore them.

This book is based on lectures I have given to aspiring novelists at various writers' conferences. The talks were followed by questions and discussion, and these contacts have helped me to recognize and deal with most of the problems which face the new writer.

No single chapter can be isolated because the craft of the novel demands so much overlapping and interweaving of ideas. Characterisation, for instance, is discussed under Theme, Viewpoint, Planning, Dialogue, Construction and The Mechanics of Improvement, as well as under its own chapter-heading. I would not wish it otherwise; a creative enterprise cannot be separated into rigid compartments.

To anyone with a gift for imaginative writing I can only say: read the following chapters, take what you feel is valid, and make a start on your novel without delay. It's a tremendous challenge, demanding and exhausting, but you will find in the work itself – quite apart from getting it published – a depth of satisfaction you never dreamed possible.

Dianne Doubtfire, Ventnor, 1978

1

Theme

"The theme of art is the theme of life itself."
Lawrence Durrell

A novel is a story about people. The novelist creates imaginary characters and involves them in dramatic situations of his own choosing. What is his motivation?

I think he tells his story to illustrate a theme that concerns him. Writers need to express their ideas and be understood; in other words, they need to communicate. The theme is usually the basis of the book and so I have chosen it as a starting point.

Theme is often confused with Plot. The theme is the *subject* of the novel (e.g. loneliness, revenge, betrayal, self-discovery) and can usually be expressed in one word, or at least in one sentence. The plot is the action of the story and would take much longer to summarise.

The structure of the novel is based on conflict. The outcome may be happy, but there must be a basic problem in order to set the plot in motion. People, as we know only too well, are inclined to create difficulties for themselves and for others. It is those difficulties, together with their extensions and solutions, which make the novel a readable entertainment. If the themes of the finest books were to be expressed in one word, that word would often be a sombre one, but this does not in any way imply that the story itself need be weighted on the side of gloom; it means that a novel cannot exist without conflict. Contented people make very dull characters in fiction. You have only to imagine yourself in a restaurant with a happy couple on one side, calmly chatting together, and on the other side two people engaged in a furious argument: you know which pair you would find the more absorbing!

What, then, will your story be *about*? What are you trying to say? A novel is not a series of incidents, however engaging; nor is it an autobiography; nor a true story – though it may be based on truth. I think it is essential to choose a theme (or maybe it chooses you) which has concerned you for many years. You can't expect to write a good novel – except perhaps a very light and superficial one – unless the subject is of great importance to you. In his book *The*

1

Wild Garden, Angus Wilson says: "*. . . the impulse to write a novel comes from a momentary unified vision of life.*" For many of us this may seem too exalted a view. We may only wish to tell our story, saying in effect: "This is how it was – make what you like of it." Nevertheless, if we have no compulsive reason for choosing that particular story, there may well be a hollow ring to it, however expert the craftsmanship. Dreads and longings drive us to write, and yet, as we explore them more deeply, changing them to create a powerful fiction, they become in some mysterious way more acceptable in our own lives. This can be a rewarding and curative experience, not only for the writer, but for those readers with similar concerns.

Everything that has happened to you – especially in your childhood – will affect your writing today, and perhaps your sufferings will prove to be of the greatest value. What you write today will affect the person you are tomorrow, and the person you are tomorrow will affect what you write the day after that. The person you are and the books you write are one and the same thing.

Beware, however, of attempting a novel about your own eventful life; there is the danger of too much fact and too little fiction. Many first novels are to some degree autobiographical – my own was no exception – but if you want to draw on direct personal experience, be sure to create imaginary characters and events, even though some of them are based on reality. I hesitate to offer this warning because nobody wants to be told what to write or what not to write, but many people do not understand that a true story of their adventures, however intriguing, will not make a *novel*, although it might become a splendid autobiography if the events are of sufficient general interest.

Never be afraid of a theme that upsets you. Tolstoy said: "*One ought only to write when one leaves a piece of one's flesh in the inkpot each time one dips one's pen.*" This advice is enough to make many a potential novelist think twice about his vocation, but the compulsive writer certainly stands a better chance of success. The more passion and dedication we bring to our work, the more likely we are to capture and keep our readers' attention. Besides, the compulsive writer slaves at his chapters in the early morning or late at night, perseveres in spite of all discouragements, and knows that he will carry on writing so long as he can hold a pen.

I think it is a mistake to reserve a pet theme until you are more accomplished. You will benefit by writing on the subject that most absorbs you, and even if your first novel is never published (every craftsman must expect to serve an apprenticeship) you will have laid firm foundations for your future work.

Sometimes it is difficult to formulate a theme at the outset, but so long as you have a rough idea of the story you want to tell, and feel deeply about it, the theme will clarify as the book evolves. In some cases the whole novel is triggered off by a simple scene in your mind. The image of a man and a woman playing chess on a seashore was the sparking point of my fourth novel, *The Flesh is Strong*. At the time, I had no idea who they were but the picture was strangely significant. The theme may not be uppermost in your mind when you first begin to conceive the idea for your story but I think you should cherish and nurture it as the book progresses. Keep asking yourself the question: "What am I trying to *say*?" even though the story itself will make increasing demands on your attention. You must tell an absorbing tale but you should also preserve your theme, however well concealed.

When you take up your pen to write a novel you move into a new arena. There is a constant change of scene and atmosphere and there is a development of character, not only for the people in your book, but for yourself. You must plunge fearlessly into that new world, see it, smell it, feel it. Hence the importance of a theme that involves you – even to the point of obsession.

Search always for that quality of "eternal truth" which underlies every contemporary situation. The girl at the bus stop in a frayed jersey and jeans can be suffering as deeply as Desdemona, and for similar reasons. The strongest themes are ageless, classless, universal.

2

Viewpoint

"It's not only a question of the artist's looking into himself but also
of his looking into others with the experience he has of himself. He
writes with sympathy because he feels that the other man is like him."
Georges Simenon

Having decided on your theme you must consider the question
of viewpoint. If this isn't properly understood, the whole edifice of
your novel can disintegrate.

You will have three or four main characters but there is usually
one who stands out as the central figure and you should know at
the outset who this is going to be. Ask yourself whose story it is.
The answer to this question is vital for the planning of your book.
There may be two or more characters vying for supremacy, but if
you consider which of them most commands your sympathy, I
think you will find the solution. Let's suppose you are planning a
novel about a man and a woman who are in conflict over his
decision to climb a dangerous mountain. If you believe that we
must all "do our own thing" even if it causes distress to those we
love, then you would write the book from the man's angle. If, on
the other hand, you think it is selfish and misguided to inflict
suffering in this way you would be likely to choose the woman,
with whom you sympathise. I have not forgotten the role of the so-
called anti-hero, but for your first book I think you would do well
to choose as your key character the kind of person you admire,
even though you might find a great deal to criticise in the way he
handles his affairs.

The four most usual approaches to the problem of viewpoint
are as follows:

1) First person singular.
2) Third person, from the viewpoint of several characters.
3) Third person, from the viewpoint of one character only.
4) The narrator.

Let's consider them one by one:

1) *First person singular*

In this case it is "I" all the way, seen through the eyes of one
character only. Nothing can be known or seen unless it is known or

seen by this person, except indirectly when someone else informs him/her about it.

This is perhaps the easiest way to write a novel because you can readily identify with an "I" character. Nevertheless, there are obvious limitations; the plot must be carefully planned to avoid the need for episodes that occur when your key person is not present. And of course this method is unsuitable if the central character would be incapable of writing the book you are giving him credit for. Here is a quotation from Alberto Moravia, widely regarded as the foremost Italian contemporary novelist: *"The first person is a vehicle that allows for an infinite widening and deepening of the novel. For while it is very difficult, and often boring, to make a third-person character say more than the scope of his actions permits, and above all to make him say it without implying an indiscreet intervention by the author, it is very easy and entirely legitimate for a first-person character to give himself over to reflections, reasonings and the rest."* (*Man as an End.*)

2) *Third person*

This is the most usual method. The characters are seen objectively and identified as "he" or "she", but three or four main figures are chosen as "viewpoint" characters. This means that the author allows himself to get inside their minds, to know exactly what they are thinking and feeling. This will not apply to any of the other people in the story, whose voices are heard and actions observed, from the outside only, by the "viewpoint" characters.

It is extremely important, in my opinion, not to change viewpoint in mid-chapter or at least in mid-scene. If this is done there is a sense of instability and fragmentation. Many leading writers shift viewpoint in this way but I still maintain that it can weaken the narrative. The reader identifies with the viewpoint character, seeing the room, the particular angle of things as they lie, the other people in the room, the whole situation, as *he* sees them. If, however, the reader is obliged to change his centre of vision from time to time and re-adjust to a new viewpoint, his attention is diverted and there is a loss of unity. I can only give you my personal opinion on this controversial matter, and ask you to consider it with care.

If you begin your novel, for example, with a quarrel between a husband and wife at the breakfast table, I think you should decide whose viewpoint to take and keep to it throughout the chapter. If you choose the wife you can describe her thoughts and feelings, but not her husband's. Everything that occurs will be seen through her eyes, and although she can see him and hear what he says (and you, as the author, will describe this), she cannot know what is in his mind. You must therefore not permit yourself, in this section, to disclose anything about the husband which the wife does not know.

In Chapter 2, perhaps, the husband's viewpoint will be taken and then you can reveal *his* thoughts. In Chapter 3 another person may become the "viewpoint" character, and in Chapter 4 the wife might be chosen again, depending on the development of the plot.

To clarify the point still further, here is an example:

> Margaret glared at her husband across the breakfast table. He was wearing his blue silk dressing-gown and his face was still flushed with sleep.
>
> "Why are you looking so morose?" she said. She knew this would be sure to make him more so, but a well-known demon goaded her.
>
> "I'm not looking morose."
>
> "Yes, you are." She wanted a row, to clear the air after the long argument of the previous night.

This is correct, keeping strictly to Margaret's viewpoint. The following is not so strong:

> "Why are you looking so morose?" she said. She knew this would be sure to make him more so, but a well-known demon goaded her.
>
> "I'm not looking morose." He glared back at her, hating the narrow curve of her mouth under its gloss of crimson lipstick.
>
> "Yes, you are." She wanted a row, to clear the air after the long argument of the previous night. He, on the other hand, wanted to avoid one at all costs.

The two offending phrases, of course, are "hating the narrow curve of her mouth under its gloss of crimson lipstick" and "He, on the other hand, wanted to avoid one at all costs." These are his thoughts, which he had not voiced.

Here is another example:

> In the dark street the girl said, "Hello, Sugar! Have you got a match?"
>
> He hurried by, trying to analyse his feelings – a strange mixture of disgust, compassion, even regret.
>
> When he had turned the corner she took out a silver lighter and lit a cigarette.

This is inadvisable because the man has been chosen as the viewpoint character and yet we see the girl after he has turned the corner of the street. You may argue that it is quite legitimate because the author has an omniscient view of all his characters, but I think it is wise to avoid the shifting viewpoint, at least in your first novel.

One further point may need clarification – the question of viewpoint when nobody is present on the scene. Suppose you want to give a bird's eye picture of a village to show its setting in the countryside. You will then describe it from your own angle, as the author who has invented it. But if you want to swoop down from the sky, as it were, and describe a particular cottage in your village where, in the living-room, a young woman is waiting for a vital telephone call, you will then be well advised to see the room from *her* point of view, revealing her feelings about the expected call, her hopes and fears as they concern the story. She is presumably a key character in the novel or you would not have focused attention on that particular cottage and that particular girl.

To sum up, if none of your characters is present, you, as the author, will express your own view of the scene. Otherwise you will be inside the mind of your chosen character, but using, of course, your own individual style as a writer to describe what occurs.

3) *Third person, but from the viewpoint of one character only*

This is a sound method, making for strength and solidity, but there are, of course, the same limitations as for the first person singular: nothing can happen which is not witnessed by or reported to your key character.

4) *The narrator*

The story is told in the first person by someone who is not closely involved. For instance, a staid old bachelor might describe the tempestuous love-life of his nephew. This story would obviously be much more powerful and dramatic if it was related in the first person by the nephew himself. The narrator technique is perhaps more suited to a leisurely or humorous tale.

You might need to experiment before reaching a final decision on your own approach. Your choice will depend on the kind of novelist you are and on the demands of your story.

Nina Bawden once said in a lecture: "You know people better in a novel than in real life because you know what people think – not just what they *say* they think." You will have to decide which of your characters are to reveal their true thoughts – the viewpoint characters – and which will only be permitted to "*say* what they think". It's an absorbing problem.

3

Planning

"What irks me is the trickiness of planning, the combining of effects, all the inner contrivances which yet belong to Art, since the effect of the style depends on them exclusively."
Gustave Flaubert

Planning is a personal matter. Some people do very little and plunge right in; some write reams of notes before beginning the actual book; some plan only in their minds. If you're a paper planner a large, loose-leaf notebook will be useful. Perhaps you have already written down an idea for a theme, the name of a character, a possible scene or a title. You will also need pencils and jotting pads placed at strategic points in the house so that wherever you are you can write down an idea or a phrase the instant it strikes you. You may think you will remember it, but later it can elude you.

A notebook and torch on the bedside table are a must for me; I'm a great believer in the power of the subconscious. If I concentrate on a problem just before I fall asleep I often find it has been solved for me during the night. Without a piece of paper to receive my sleepy scrawl the new ideas might vanish without trace. We all have our different sources of inspiration but I think it is a mistake to rely on memory to preserve ideas. A cassette-recorder can be useful but for that vital hasty note perhaps there is really nothing to match an old envelope and a stub of pencil.

For me it is the characters who occupy the most space in my preliminary notebook. (*Dora bites her nails; Charles hates cats; Eileen can't resist buying bracelets . . .*) Take your main character: the first thing is to choose a suitable name. You may find it difficult to begin until you are satisfied that the name you have chosen is exactly right. A telephone directory might help, although of course you will change and interchange the names until you find the one that fits. If you can discover it without such artificial means, so much the better. Don't ignore the value of nicknames; we all use them and they add warmth and authenticity to your story.

When you have the name, you could write down his year of birth, and his age at the time the story opens. You should know a great deal about your main characters, even though you only use a fraction of your knowledge. Decide on the parents, education, appearance, temperament, religion, politics. . . . You should know their tastes in music, films, food and holidays. You should be able to gauge their replies to your questions. In other words you must know them thoroughly – better even than you know anyone in real life, because you will understand their secret fears and hopes, their worst and noblest motives. They will grow clearer to you as you write about them, just as a new friend reveals himself a little more at every meeting. Sometimes they will surprise you by behaving unpredictably, as real people do. When people are under stress they reveal their true nature; the seemingly strong expose their weaknesses, and *vice versa*. How will your characters react? What will they say and do when driven by love, hatred, fear, ambition, despair . . .?

In your notebook you will also want to jot down ideas about the setting for your novel, the real and imaginary places you will introduce. An old road atlas may be useful here, not only to pinpoint actual venues but to give you ideas for place-names. Your notebook could contain sketch-maps of imaginary villages, plans of rooms, drawings of people: anything, in fact, that will help you to picture the details of your novel more clearly.

An important aspect of planning is the time-span of the book. Is it going to cover a week, a year, ten years, or a lifetime? You will need to think carefully about the dates, ages of characters, and any actual events which might affect your story. The Second World War can be a problem if your novel includes those years; you can't have an able-bodied Englishman of twenty-eight growing sweet-peas in 1943!

You will probably jot down a variety of dramatic episodes as they come to you – snatches of dialogue, descriptions of people or places, ideas for new characters, etc. Make rough notes and sort them out at leisure. Those sudden flashes of insight are beyond price. Heaven knows where they come from, but I think we should receive them with joy, respect and gratitude. Without them, no novel of quality would ever be written. Keep your notebook handy; it will put you in the mood to write again when you are in the doldrums.

The length of a "straight" novel can be anything from 60,000 to 100,000 words, but 70–80,000 is a good average and in any case your book will find its own length as it develops.

The length of each chapter will depend on the length of the

novel; there are no rules. If they are of uneven lengths, let them be arranged with a sense of balance. Don't, for instance, have five chapters of 4,000 words, then one of 1,000, and then all the rest about 2,000. Let them hang like a fringe – of varying lengths perhaps, but none out of harmony with the rest.

A good basic plan would be 30 chapters of approximately 2,500 words each. You can divide a chapter into sections with a double space where necessary, but beware of asterisks; they can give your book a rather dated appearance. You might decide that you don't want chapters at all, but I wouldn't advise you to do away with them in your first novel.

In 1954 I attended the annual Writers' Summer School at Swanwick in Derbyshire where the late Winston Clewes was lecturing on The Novel. After his talk I asked him the following question – one which might be troubling you at this very moment. "I want to start a novel," I said, "but it's all just a muddle in my mind. How can I sort it out?"

His answer was invaluable. He advised me to write the numbers 1–30 down the left-hand side of a sheet of foolscap paper and against number 1 to jot down a note about a possible opening. Against number 30, one could write an idea for an ending, and against various other numbers (perhaps only a few at first) brief notes on some highspots in the story.

After years of indecision and apprehension, this advice made me concentrate all my attention, first of all, on the opening, and then to look ahead to a possible climax. I found that the definite concept of a beginning and an end brought the intervening stretch within manageable bounds and made the whole project far less intimidating. I found it was the numbers 1–5 which helped me most. I made a note of my opening scene after number 1, then, after 2 and 3, I planned possible developments from that scene. When I actually began to write I discovered that my plan for Chapter 2 was wrong; I needed an extra chapter to consolidate the first. This meant that my proposed Chapter 2 became the actual Chapter 3, and 3 became 4. If you keep jotting down notes on your foolscap chapter-sheet it will give you an idea of the direction the story might take, and you will find yourself led on by your notes until the novel gains such solidity that you no longer require them. When I lectured on the craft of the novel at the Writers' Summer School thirteen years after talking to Winston Clewes, I passed on the "1–30" method and it has been of great value to many potential novelists. Several of them have told me that it started them off on books which have since been accepted.

Try to plan a strong backbone for your book and work towards a powerful climax, but always be prepared to alter your plans if the characters demand it. It doesn't matter in the least if the whole scheme changes as you write; in fact it must surely change. People behave as they do because they are as they are, and until you know your characters you cannot plan their actions with any finality. Your climax might work out quite differently from the way you first envisaged it. Work steadily from one scene to the next and the muddle will gradually unravel, as a tangle of string will unravel if handled with patience and confidence. People in conflict are vital to the planning of any novel. But more of that later.

The planning of each separate chapter is of great importance but it is only when the narrative is strongly under way that you can decide finally where the chapter endings will be. You might use the break between chapters to bridge a gap in time or space, to change viewpoint, to launch your story in a new direction or to introduce a flashback. Whatever the reason, be sure to devise chapter endings which compel your reader to turn the page.

A novel, in my view, should be fluid from the start – a voyage of discovery, full of surprises. If you, the author, are continually surprised, there is much more likelihood that the reader will be. I seldom know the ending until I reach the final few chapters – in one book (*Kick a Tin Can*) I didn't know it until I was writing the last page! Planning is a valuable preliminary, but it is only when the book itself is progressing that the muddle really begins to sort itself out. Get on with the writing, I would say. Don't be afraid of it. If you linger at the planning stage you may never start the book at all.

4

Setting

"The author must know his countryside, whether real or imaginary, like his hand. . . ."
Robert Louis Stevenson

Where is it all going to happen?

The choice of settings will obviously depend on your characters and your story, but the scenes you choose will have such an effect on the atmosphere you evoke that they deserve very careful consideration. You can imbue the reader with a sense of horror, mystery, isolation, peace, violence, sorrow, gaiety, or any one of a thousand other moods, simply by your choice of scene.

Read the following and see how the swift change of impressions affects your mood. *A train crash in the snow; a millionaire's gold bathroom; a long bus queue on a wet night; the burnt-out shell of a cottage in a bluebell wood; a Cup Final stadium after a decisive goal. . . .* You have only to note the evocative nature of those simple phrases to realise the limitless choice of venue at your command and the power you might wield with a detailed and keenly-felt description.

Choose for your locations a country (or countries) that you know, otherwise there will be something missing from the atmosphere, however careful your research may have been. How could you describe the smell of the Paris Metro if you hadn't been there, or the discarded tickets that litter the exits? No one who hasn't lived in the tropics could know about the sickly sweating silence in the night when a power failure has stopped the fan. And who would believe how endlessly the people in England talk about the weather? Books and travel films are no substitute for experience. Study the opening of *Balthazar*, the second book of Lawrence Durrell's *Alexandria Quartet*:

> Landscape-tones: brown to bronze, steep skyline, low cloud, pearl ground with shadowed oyster and violet reflections. The lion-dust of desert: prophets' tombs turned to zinc and copper at sunset on the ancient lake. Its huge sand-faults like watermarks from the air; green and citron giving to gunmetal, to a single plum-dark sail, moist, palpitant: sticky-winged nymph.

What an eye for colour! And how could he possibly have written that description without personal knowledge?

Here is a simpler kind of scene-setting from *Travels with My Aunt* by Graham Greene:

> I found Aunt Augusta sitting alone in the centre of the large and shabby salon, filled with green velvet chairs and marble mantelpieces. She had not bothered to remove the suitcase, which lay open and empty on the floor. There were traces of tears in her eyes. I turned on the dim lights of the dusty chandelier, and my aunt gave me an uncertain smile.

Note how the description of the room is combined with the image of Aunt Augusta; setting, character, action, thought and dialogue are inseparable. No description of a place should occupy more than half a page at a stretch.

Don't attempt to describe a setting or an experience unless you have first-hand knowledge of something similar. I recently wrote a teenage novel with a hang-gliding background; my son is an instructor and I had every opportunity of making it authentic. I made the mistake, however, of writing about a flight before I had actually done it myself. It might have been acceptable to anyone who had never flown but as soon as I had a dual flight with my son I knew what was missing from the original version. It had to be scrapped.

This advice applies to foreign countries, lorry drivers' cafés, television studios, maternity wards, aircraft hangars, etc. If you haven't the inside knowledge, and can't see your way to acquiring it, then try to plan things differently. Lack of conviction is death to your novel.

If you choose for your background a small town or village that you know, you would be well advised to alter it a little and to change its name. You will not only find this approach more stimulating from a creative point of view but you will also run less danger of libel action. You can allow your characters to lunch at Harrods', which is large and impersonal, but it would be a mistake to let them eat at the one and only hotel in a village which you call by its real name and describe as it really is; the same proprietor might still be there! When you introduce an actual location, such as Lake Windermere or Piccadilly Circus, make sure that the details are authentic in relation to the time at which your action takes place.

Try to form a visual impression of your setting, whether real or imaginary, and select its most telling aspects for your description. You should be able to see the venue in your mind's eye; if it's a garden, you know where the gate is and where it leads to. You can see the trees and the flowers, the quality of light that shines through the leaves. You know what time of the year it is, what time of day, what kind of day. In other words, *you're there*! Your own little sketch-maps and diagrams, as I mentioned under Planning, can be very helpful.

Every scene is like a dream picture, a kind of hallucination deliberately envisaged and yet partly emanating from that mysterious source that feeds the imagination. It can grow out of actual experience, wishful thinking, fear, or perhaps simply from a sense of beauty or drama. Most novelists find that this visual power comes naturally, but with practice you can develop it, just as you can develop your skills in all aspects of writing.

See how Iris Murdoch, in her novel *The Sacred and Profane Love Machine*, describes a new motorway:

> David in his flight had reached the place where, so dramatically it had lately seemed to him, the chaotic brown tumbled earth of the embankment, the great curving side of the thing, rolled like volcanic lava, like a strange immobilized sea, out onto the ordinary grass of the ordinary meadow: a meadow which David had known before the coming of the motorway, where he had searched for mushrooms in previous autumns, in lost quiet golden hazes. But now already the arrested volcanic sea seemed that much less strange, seemed a little to belong to the country. The big brown flank was no longer quite brown, was misted over with patches of grass and little white daisies and red poppies and starry clumps of red and yellow pimpernel and sky-blue birds-eye.

Colour, again! And note the reference to the landscape as it used to be when David searched for mushrooms. This adds drama to the "volcanic sea".

It is important to plan your locations with a sense of balance. For instance, it would be unsatisfactory to set your first chapter in a luxury flat in New York and then switch to a remote Welsh farmhouse and stay there for the rest of the novel. But if you returned to the New York flat for the last chapter, the balance would be restored. In fact there is something very attractive about the notion of letting your story come full circle and end where it began.

There are, of course, no rules concerning the number or variety of locations; the whole novel might take place in one room, or you could have dozens of different settings. A happy compromise is perhaps the wisest choice for the new novelist. Foreign backgrounds are popular but I advise you not to worry about that; just give your story its own natural setting and concentrate on writing it with integrity and skill.

5

Characterisation

"We are not interested in the sort of objectivity that turns out machine-made collections of types and characters, but in the purely poetic capacity to represent one's own hopes, one's own fears, one's own resentments, one's own loves, in human form: to define oneself by subdividing oneself and multiplying oneself in one or a hundred creatures."

Alberto Moravia

How does one create believable characters? Whip them up out of nothing, or copy real people? The answer is neither of these alone, but a mixture of both. We must base our imaginative creations on what we know of ourselves and of the people we have met. Writers of fiction are people of many facets, and some of their characters are developments of themselves, the good and the bad magnified or tempered by a sensitive imagination.

"The novelist's job is to see and say clearly what people are." In this simple statement I think John Masters has summed up the whole art of characterisation. But *how* are we to see clearly and to say clearly? The first depends on our understanding of human nature, the second on the writing technique we acquire through study and experience.

Characters in a novel should never be taken straight from life. Apart from the risk of libel, it is artistically unsatisfactory, in that one must know one's characters completely, as one can never know a real person. No one reveals every secret experience, every hope, fear and passion to another person, however close, and it is impossible to understand a person's behaviour completely unless one knows his whole history from earliest childhood. Therefore, to put an actual person into a novel, and invent imaginary actions for him, would be to build without a sound foundation. The best way to create character is to invent the whole person in his entirety, so that all is known to you and every action is based on a temperament and background which you yourself have devised. You will then be in a position to invent behaviour for him which is not only convincing but inevitable. If you work this way, your characters grow from within themselves. If you take someone from real life you impose on him activities for which you do not understand the root

17

causes. Established writers, of course, have sometimes done this very thing, but I would certainly not advise it. Some authors add a note to the effect that all their characters are entirely fictitious and bear no resemblance to any actual persons, living or dead, but this statement carries no legal weight whatsoever. (There is a section on British libel in *The Writers' and Artists' Year Book*.)

One of your main objectives as a novelist is to make your readers care what happens to your characters; this is the secret of readability. If the reader is to care, you yourself must care, so don't be tempted to continue with a novel unless you feel an intense involvement with all your key characters. To make them true to life you must understand their motives, good and bad. If we are honest we can usually understand our own motives, so we must use ourselves as models. We know all about those subtle stabs of revenge we deal out when we've been hurt. We know the love and gratitude that wells up in response to kindness and sympathy. We know how cruelty engenders more cruelty. The novelist should be continually interrogating himself. "Why did I say that?" "Why did I do that?" "Why am I so touchy about certain things?" A study of psychology is valuable, but the best thing is to study yourself objectively and other people compassionately, so that you can see the principles of human nature at work and compose your novel accordingly. Every person alive is different, and you, as a novelist, must create more people – quite new. You can't expect it to be easy!

Why do some characters seem "cardboard"? Stilted dialogue has a lot to do with it, but I think you will also find that the cardboard character is either too good, too bad, or too predictable. Up to a point, most of us are "true to type" but there are always deviations. We often hear someone say: "I'd never have expected that of So-and-So!" A conventional person may suddenly behave wildly for no apparent reason. But if you have created the character yourself with deep involvement, you *know* the reason; you know, for example, that he had been forced into conventional channels against his will and that the time had come for him to revert to his true nature. A mean person may be extravagant in certain little ways, perhaps in an effort to compensate for secret guilt. If he is your creation you will understand, and his behaviour will carry conviction.

Another symptom of the cardboard character is that he remains the same throughout the book. In reality people change, however slightly, as a result of their experiences. There must be some sort of conversion brought about by the events you devise; the central character must develop along with the novel and acquire new attitudes – preferably wiser ones; I believe in regeneration not degeneration.

A great deal of "thinking time" – and possibly some note-taking – is required before a character can develop fully in the mind. If you feel that one of your characters is lacking in depth it is probably because you are unsure of his true nature. Unless you know your people so well that you feel you are in their presence as you write, they are unlikely to come over as flesh-and-blood creations.

How much visual description should you give? This is for you to decide but I think the modern reader prefers to picture the characters for himself, basing his impression on a few well-chosen details. E.g. In Graham Greene's *A Burnt-Out Case*, "Father Thomas's long narrow nose was oddly twisted at the end; it gave him the effect of smelling sideways at some elusive odour." And in Nina Bawden's *George Beneath a Paper Moon*, of George's grandmother: "Her face was old now, a used crumpled envelope, but a child still looked out from her eyes."

The following extracts will further illustrate the art of sketching a character in a few words:

> She always kissed him when he got home, not a conventional peck on the cheek but a light kiss full on the mouth: she had moist, wide lips and usually forgot to wear lipstick. There was always a smell that he liked at this time of day, faded perfume not yet renewed, so that it had the aura of powder or soap rather than scent. Blindfolded, he would have said, "That's Cassie."
>
> (*A Bouquet of Barbed Wire* by Andrea Newman)

> "Hey, miss," said a soft voice. "You like a cup of tea?"
> I looked up. Beside the bed stood a huge bulky figure in a plaid shirt, surmounted by a broad black head split like a ripe chestnut on a crescent of snowy teeth. Dwarfed by the enormous black paw which held it was a steaming cup.
>
> (*The L-Shaped Room* by Lynne Reid Banks)

> Sometimes when she wasn't reading her part she looked plain, in fact downright ugly: her chin had a heavy shapelessness and the lines on her forehead and neck were as if scored with a knife. When she was acting her face came to life: it wasn't so much that you forgot its blemishes as that they became endearing and exciting.
>
> (*Room at the Top* by John Braine)

When Bretherton woke, beer-flushed, with belches of discomfort, at the sound of the caddy spoon on the side of the teapot, he looked like one of those model porkers, fat and pinkish, squatting on its hind-legs with an advertisement for sausages in its lap, that you see in butchers' windows. The sausages were his fingers. They glistened, a pink-grey colour, as they grasped tremulously at each other and then at his tobacco-yellow moustache.

(Love for Lydia by H. E. Bates)

An experienced writer can sustain a lengthy description without becoming tedious:

Now she sat there, tired and comfortable, in a deep arm chair, with her feet curled up under her, looking at the pictures. She wore a long wool skirt, and expensive shoes. She was tall, slight and bony, her face was lined and hard and sweet. She had the gallant air of a woman fighting a losing battle, but nobody could guess the terms of her defeat, for she was discreet and silent about herself. She had a well-shaped mouth, curiously curved, with thin and conscious delicate lips, a careful and precise and gentle way of speech. Her hair was dyed. It had turned, in the course of nature, from brown to a miserable, mustardy yellowy fuzzy grey, and so she dyed it, back to its original brown. It was her one weak gesture, and it was a realistic one, for she did, as she had said to Frances one day some years ago, look like the Witch of Endor with it undyed. And who wants to look like *that*? she had said. It isn't fair to other people, she had said. Who could tell what vanity lay concealed in her? Certainly she always wore extremely expensive shoes. Now they were tucked under her, out of sight. . . .

(The Realms of Gold by Margaret Drabble)

I was particularly impressed by the second reference to the expensive shoes. Such repetitions can serve to highlight some special quality of a person or a place, but obviously they must be introduced with great care.

Animals, too, demand characterisation. Study this beautiful example from Iris Murdoch's *Under the Net*:

Another peculiarity of Mrs Tinckham's shop is that it is full of cats. An ever-increasing family of tabbies, sprung from one enormous matriarch, sit about upon the counter and on empty shelves, somnolent and contemplative, their amber eyes narrowed and winking in the sun, a reluctant slit of liquid in an expanse of hot fur.

You might practise characterisation by describing someone you know, choosing one thing only to clarify the personality. For instance: an old woman who wears men's shoes; a man who always taps his pipe out on the dot of 10 p.m.; a girl with no ear for music who is constantly humming popular songs off-key; a small schoolboy with thin legs whose socks are always round his ankles.

Let your characters reveal themselves gradually, as people do: appearance first, voice, mannerisms, followed by subtleties of behaviour and attitude. Let the deeper aspects emerge later, although some of them will perhaps be implied from the start; an unkind remark in the first chapter can be a pointer towards an act of brutality in the last. Keep reminding your readers (very unobtrusively) of the facts you have imparted. If you describe a woman with trembling hands, later she might have difficulty in fitting a key into a lock, and the reader will remember about the trembling hands, even though it was six chapters ago. If you portray a girl who longs for a leather jacket, you have only to press her nose against a shop window and we know what she is gazing at. As a rule it is best not to describe a person until he is actually there in the narrative; a previous build-up can sometimes be effective, but this is the exception.

When you create an evil character, know *why* he or she is evil. Reveal his confusion and unhappiness as well as his malice. To carry conviction, your characters will be a mixture of good and bad, as we all are. You will probably dislike your most beloved character from time to time, just as we dislike our friends when they display their worst selves to us.

If you analyse the people in your favourite novels, you will discover that many of them are portrayed as "larger than life". The exaggeration may not be great enough for them to be described as caricatures but they are often more eccentric or impressive than most of the folk we meet every day. Take this into account when you are creating your characters; don't be afraid of that extra helping of personality.

> When some new thought gripped his heart he went to the kitchen, his headquarters, to write it down. The white paint was scaling from the brick walls and Herzog sometimes wiped mouse droppings from the table with his sleeve, calmly wondering why field mice should have such a passion for wax and paraffin. They made holes in paraffin-sealed preserves; they gnawed birthday candles down to the wicks. A rat chewed into a package of bread, leaving the shape of its body in the layers of slices. Herzog ate the other half of the loaf spread with jam. He could share with rats too.
>
> (*Herzog* by Saul Bellow)

Sometimes a character becomes so real that he refuses to do what you have planned for him. When this happens, don't coerce him; it means you have created a real person with a will of his own and this is a marvellous moment in any novelist's life. Hold him on a light rein, as it were, giving him his head to a certain degree but ensuring that he does not stampede you out of your story. You must remain in command whilst allowing your creations to behave in accordance with the qualities you have given them. Write your scene with all the skill you have and let your instinct tell you whether or not it carries conviction. Creating imaginary characters is the core of novel-writing – and the possibilities are endless.

6

Dialogue

"The dialogue is generally the most agreeable part of a novel, but it is so only so long as it tends in some way to the telling of the main story."

Anthony Trollope

You cannot, of course, put down everything your characters would really say in the given circumstances. You have only to listen to five minutes of true-life dialogue to realise that normal conversation would be unbearably tedious in a novel. You must prune and edit your speeches, directing them towards what is essential for the forward movement of your story and the delineation of character. You might argue that to delineate the character of a bore you must allow him to *be* a bore, but the trouble with this is that the reader would find him wearisome, as well. It is possible to show that a person is boring without making your dialogue uninteresting. Humour can help, and conflict, but if you find it difficult, take heart from Gustave Flaubert: *"I've never in my life written anything more difficult than these conversations full of trivialities. This scene at the inn may take me three months for all I know. I could weep sometimes, I feel so helpless. . . ."*

Every line of dialogue must be precisely tailored for the person concerned. In a good novel you can usually tell who is speaking even from isolated sentences; everyone has his individual choice of words, and manner of framing remarks. Here for instance, are twenty different ways of saying Yes. Imagine that a man has been asked to close a door which he has just left ajar: Yes; Yeah; O.K.; Oky-doke; Right; Certainly; Of course; Indeed; Indeedy; Will do; Sure thing; All right; If you say so; Why not?; Delighted; Yep; *So* sorry; Huh; Righty-ho. Or just a silence to denote the absence of a negative response. You should know which of these replies any of your characters would use, depending, of course, on the person who made the request. The same man might easily say "Delighted" to one woman and "Huh" to another!

Study the beginning of *The Graduate* by the American author Charles Webb, and note the contrast of personalities:

Benjamin Braddock graduated from a small Eastern college on a day in June. Then he flew home. The following evening a party was given for him by his parents. By eight o'clock most of the guests had arrived but Benjamin had not yet come down from his room. His father called up from the foot of the stairs but there was no answer. Finally he hurried up the stairs and to the end of the hall.

"Ben?" he said, opening his son's door.

"I'll be down later," Benjamin said.

"Ben, the guests are all here," his father said. "They're all waiting."

"I said I'll be down later."

Mr Braddock closed the door behind him. "What is it," he said.

Benjamin shook his head and walked to the window.

"What is it, Ben."

"Nothing."

"Then why don't you come on down and see your guests."

Benjamin didn't answer.

"Ben?"

"Dad," he said, turning around, "I have some things on my mind right now."

"What things."

"Just some things."

"Well can't you tell me what they are?"

"No."

Mr Braddock continued frowning at his son a few more moments, glanced at his watch, then looked back at Benjamin. "Ben, these are our friends down there," he said. "My friends. Your mother's friends. You owe them a little courtesy."

"Tell them I have to be alone right now."

In this passage, it is worth noting too, how the simplicity of the narrative, in conjunction with the taut dialogue, helps to build up the tension of the situation.

How much dialogue should you introduce into your book? There is no easy guide-line but in this age of television drama, when we are all used to hearing the characters talking nearly all the time, I think you need quite a large proportion – say thirty per cent. But do keep it crisp and entertaining; good fiction dialogue contains no inessentials. For guidance, analyse the dialogue in any successful novel of the kind you wish to write.

Always read your speeches aloud; this helps to reveal the faults. Avoid the stilted "he did not" and "she would not" when "he didn't" and "she wouldn't" would be normal speech. Be careful not to make your characters speak as if they were reading an essay or addressing a meeting. This is a special danger if you are making somebody voice one of your own pet theories; it is a temptation to climb on to the soap box with him and enjoy the sound of your own voice.

As a rule, keep speeches short; people seldom talk for long without interruption unless they have a captive audience. *"No character should utter much above a dozen words at a breath – unless the writer can justify to himself a longer flood of speech by the speciality of the occasion."* (Anthony Trollope)

In the following extract (the opening of *The Pumpkin Eater* by Penelope Mortimer), there is a good example of a long speech, totally acceptable in this context on account of the "speciality of the occasion" –in this case a captive audience.

"Well," I said, "I will try. I honestly will try to be honest with you, although I suppose really what you're more interested in is my not being honest, if you see what I mean."

The doctor smiled slightly.

"When I was a child my mother had a wool drawer. It was the bottom drawer in a chest in the dining-room and she kept every scrap of wool she had in it. You know, bits from years ago, jumpers she'd knitted me when I was two. Some of the bits were only a few inches long. Well, this drawer was filled with wool, all colours, and whenever it was a wet afternoon she used to make me tidy her wool drawer. It's perfectly obvious why I tell you this. There was no point in tidying the drawer. The wool was quite useless. You couldn't have knitted a tea-cosy out of that wool, I mean without enormous patience. She just made me sort it out for something to do, like they make prisoners dig holes and fill them up again. You do see what I mean, don't you?"

"You would like to be something useful," he said sadly. "Like a tea-cosy."

"It can't be as easy as that."

"Oh no. It's not at all easy. But there are other things you can make from wool."

"Such as?"

"Hot water bottle covers," he said promptly.

"We don't use hot water bottles. Balls you can make, for babies. Or small golliwogs."

"The point you are trying to make is that tidying the wool is a useless and probably impossible task?"

"Yes."

"But you are a human being. The consequences of your . . . muddle are more grave. The comparison, you see, is not a true one."

"Well, it's how it feels to me," I said.

"When you cry, is that how it feels? Hopeless?"

"I just want to open my mouth and cry. I want to cry, and not think."

"But you can't cry for the rest of your life."

"No."

"You can't worry for the rest of your life."

"No."

"What do you worry *about*, Mrs Armitage?"

"Dust," I said.

"I'm sorry?"

"Dust. You know? Dust."

"Oh," he said, and wrote for a while on a long piece of paper. Then he sat back, folded his hands and said, "Tell me about it."

Note how the short exchanges which follow the longer speech serve to launch us into the story. Mrs Armitage is introduced and her serious problem established, but the touch is light, and we are permitted to smile as we sympathise. Tension increases and we want to read on.

Don't have people talking in a void; decide where they are and what they are doing while they converse. In the previous extract there is no description of the room but we know that Mrs Armitage is with a doctor and that he is sitting at his desk. A page or so later we are given a more detailed picture: "I stared at him, silhouetted against the net-curtained window of the consulting room. I heard the tick of the clock, the hiss of the gas fire."

This enables us to see the doctor and the room through her eyes, hear the sounds through her ears. We are there with her.

Beware of what I call "ping-pong dialogue". Sentences are tossed backwards and forwards with mechanical rhythm. The ball never hits the net or bounces onto the floor. In actual conversation people are continually breaking off, interrupting one another, changing the subject, answering the wrong question, becoming embarrassed, losing their tempers. . . . Remember that a great deal of what people say is designed to *conceal* the truth rather than reveal it.

It is best to avoid dialect, as it presents difficulties to readers from other parts of the country, but different vernaculars can be suggested by choice of vocabulary and turn of phrase without too many apostrophes to signify missing letters.

It is, of course, perfectly in order to use ungrammatical speech for a character who would normally speak that way. It is not only in order, it is essential. The same applies to strong language. You must suit the language to the character. You are showing people as they *are*, not as you might like them to be, and no matter how much you may disapprove of swearing, you wouldn't make your builder's mate say "Damn" when he drops a brick on his toe! A novelist must allow his creations to use their own authentic vocabulary, but he is naturally free to exercise his personal discrimination in the choice of theme and characters in the first place.

Don't be afraid of the simple "he said" and "she said". It is the sign of the amateur to search for alternatives when they are not really necessary: "he expostulated"; "she gushed"; "he averred", etc. "Said" can be used a great deal more than one would expect, without disturbing the reader. In my Penguin copy of *England Made Me* by Graham Greene, I found no less than sixteen "saids" on one page, but you would never notice them unless you were on the look-out. It is only necessary to use alternatives if you want to express a particular manner of speech, such as "whispered" or "shouted".

If it is clear who is speaking, just set down the speech on its own. Beware, however, of going on for too long in this way; we all know how annoying it is to have to count back to see who started!

It is best to begin a fresh paragraph for every new speech by a different character, but if the same person carries on talking after an action *of his own* you should continue on the same line. For example:

> "I'm sorry," said Ruth, without looking at him. She closed the suitcase and fastened the bulky leather strap. "I shan't change my mind. I'm going to ring for a taxi."

If, however, the man had spoken it would be printed as follows:

> "I'm sorry," said Ruth, without looking at him. She closed the suitcase and fastened the bulky leather strap.
> "Please – darling –"
> "I shan't change my mind," she said. "I'm going to ring for a taxi."

Note the addition of "she said" in this instance, to improve the flow.

It is a matter of choice as to whether one uses single or double quotation marks, and most publishers have their own preference. If one employs double quotation marks for dialogue, then single ones should be used for quotes within a speech, and *vice versa*. It is better not to use quotation marks for unspoken thoughts, even though they take a clear verbal form in the character's mind.

Writers vary in their treatment of this problem but I think the meaning is most clearly expressed by beginning the thought sequence with a capital letter. E.g. *She thought, How can I tell him the truth?* There is no better way of learning these techniques, including the lay-out of dialogue on the page, than by studying the published work of good modern novelists. I emphasise "modern" because you *must* be up-to-date in your approach to the craft if you want to interest a publisher.

7

Working Arrangements

"Write as often as possible, not with the idea at once of getting
into print, but as if you were learning an instrument."
J. B. Priestley

Working arrangements, like planning, are a very personal
matter, and I can only pass on a few tips that might help you to
organise your writing life more effectively.

Finding the Time

Somehow you will need to find at least an hour a day for
regular writing; three would be better. If you have a full-time job
(and I include, of course, a home to look after) you might have to
decide whether you are a lark or an owl, and utilise the early
morning or the late hours accordingly. I'm a lark and when my son
was small I got up every morning at 4.30. I huddled over the kit-
chen boiler and wrote for two hours, until he awoke. Getting up is
always difficult for me but once I have washed my face in cold
water and made some tea, the actual time of day doesn't seem
important. What *is* important is the progress of my book. I still get
up at 5.45 a.m., having trained myself to sleep for only six or seven
hours, and if time is your problem I strongly recommend you to try
it.

It is better to arrange short regular periods of work than long
spasmodic stints. If you are going to complete a novel it is essential
to get into the habit of regular work. The best practical approach is
to decide how long you can spare each day and choose the most
convenient time. Having decided, stick to it with great self-
discipline. You might have to cut down on reading, watch less
television, or curtail some social pleasures. Friends and relations
will have to learn to respect your working schedule and avoid in-
trusion when you are writing. You will probably be unpopular
(until your novel is published!) with those who do not understand
how much hard work goes into a book. Some sacrifices will be
necessary if you are going to become a novelist, but you are
probably prepared to make them if you have read as far as this.

It takes me two years to write a novel. If I produce 2000 words
in my six-hour working day I am overjoyed. A general average is

about 750. This would imply that I could write a book in about five months, but a month's work might have to be re-written in the light of some unexpected development of character or plot. Whole chapters can prove irrelevant and have to be scrapped or reframed. Nevertheless, I am convinced that none of the time spent battling with your book is ever wasted; your mistakes are an integral part of the job. Few writers can produce satisfactory work without constant trial and error.

Write new material when you are fresh and leave the revision till later. If you finish your day's stint at a point when you know what is coming next you will be able to begin again more easily. Some people even leave their work in mid-sentence to simplify the next day's start. I like to read over the last page I wrote; I can always find something to improve, and the involvement with correction usually puts me in the mood to forge ahead.

Writers, like most creative artists, will always look for any excuse not to start work, from reading the paper to baking a cake. The solution to this is to choose a definite starting time and let nothing (with certain exceptions) stop you from sitting down to work at that precise moment. I wish I could claim to follow my own advice, but when I *do* manage it I know by the results – in output and in satisfaction – that it is the best plan. There are countless people with all the talent required to produce a brilliant novel, but they lack that other essential – the ability to work regularly and with concentration in spite of difficulties. I sometimes think that self-discipline is an integral part of talent. Certainly talent can be tragically wasted without it. I use a simple slogan to get me out of a lazy mood. It consists of four words and it seldom fails to galvanise me into immediate action: *It Won't Write Itself!* Laziness is a habit, and so is hard work. Hard work produces a thickening pile of chapters which gradually acquires *weight.* A book is being written, and you are happy.

A working lunch can be a great incentive. Prepare a tray of sandwiches with a glass of wine or a mug of coffee, take it to your workroom and busy yourself with your novel while you munch and sip. You might well find yourself launched on a whole afternoon of creative effort.

Never talk to *anyone* about your novel before you begin to write it. Your book is a voyage of discovery and if you first discover it verbally you can destroy that secret anticipation and make your work more difficult – or even impossible. *"The precarious ride from the first clue to the beginning of the Rough may last many weeks. On the way I have to renew my vows of silence. In the rising excitement, with the dream unrolling in my head, it is too easy to talk. And talking is fatal." (Pen to Paper* by Pamela Frankau)

Once you have finished a chapter, by all means seek the honest opinions of fellow writers. But on no account allow yourself to be dejected – or encouraged – by the comments of uninitiated relatives and friends.

A Place of Work

If you are lucky enough to have a satisfactory study, skip this section. If not, maybe you have a store room, spare room or bedroom which could be fixed up with a table, a good light and a portable heater, if need be. The ideal, I think, is a garden chalet where one can be isolated from noise and interruption and from those niggling problems of everyday life which can so easily destroy your fictional world. This, however, is a pipe-dream for many, as it used to be for me; we can only do our best to arrange things to our liking.

You may be one of those fortunate people who can write with the radio on at full blast, two small children wrestling on the floor at your feet, and a pneumatic drill in the street outside your window. I'm not, and my output has increased enormously since I acquired an outdoor chalet. Nevertheless, I worked for fifteen years in kitchens and bedrooms, and you will somehow find the time and the place to write your book if you set about it with real determination.

Accessories

You *can*, if absolutely necessary, manage without a typewriter, provided you have your novel typed when it is ready for the publisher, but you really should acquire one as soon as possible. If your handwriting is anything like mine, you will need to type out each chapter as you go along in order to see what you have written. Then you can make improvements, re-type, make more improvements, and gradually get your work into shape. Two-finger typing is all you need, but touch-typing, they tell me, can make your life as a novelist a great deal simpler.

There are a few other items you will need for your desk in addition to a typewriter. They are the obvious tools of the trade but I will list them here, if only to whet your appetite for the task ahead: notebook; pencils; ball-point or fountain pen; pencil sharpener; paper clips; typing paper (A4 in the UK/$8\frac{1}{2}''$ x $11''$ in the

USA) and carbon paper; typing eraser; correction strips or fluid, such as Tipp-Ex; typewriter cleaning brush; scrap paper. (Offcuts of scrap paper are often available cheaply at a local printers' or newspaper office.)

You may decide to send out your completed novel to a professional typist rather than battle with the job yourself, in which case it is advisable to choose a typist by personal recommendation. In any case, ask for an estimate. Some typists include paper and postage in the estimated charge and some don't, so be sure to find out about this in advance.

The following reference books will be of great value: *The Concise Oxford Dictionary* (or *The Shorter Oxford Dictionary*, preferably in two volumes) or *Webster's New Collegiate Dictionary*, *Funk & Wagnalls Standard College Dictionary* or *The Random House Dictionary*; *Roget's Thesaurus of English Words and Phrases*; Fowler's *Modern English Usage* or Strunk and White's *Elements of Style*; and the latest edition of *The Writers' and Artists' Year Book* in Britain or *The Writer's Handbook*, *The Literary Market Place* or *The Writer's Market* in America. An encyclopaedia is always useful but the Public Reference Library will suffice for research when you are writing a "straight" novel. In any case the librarian is usually very helpful and will advise you on all sources of information.

Unless you're a natural loner, don't overlook the advantages of belonging to a Writers' Group. (You can find out about the nearest one from your local library.) Apart from the criticism you will receive – some of which will be valid, honest and constructive – there is a lot to be said for regular meetings with other writers: if you are inclined to be lazy you will have an added incentive to keep working, the sharing of problems can be a comfort, and you will probably find at least one valuable friend who is on your wavelength and with whom you can exchange ideas about your craft. Writers' Circles come in for a certain amount of criticism – and even ridicule – but I know I could not have achieved success so soon, if at all, without the advice I received from my local Circle when I was a raw beginner. I have many friends who say the same.

8

The First Chapter

"Yet even then I hesitated, as if warned by the instinct of self-
preservation from venturing on a distant and toilsome journey into a
land full of intrigue and revolutions. But it had to be done."
Joseph Conrad

You might be surprised to find this chapter nearly halfway
through the book, but I think it is wise to consider all aspects of
planning, scene and characterisation before you write "Chapter
One" on that first blank sheet of paper.

Perhaps the most useful advice I can give is to start with a
character (or characters) in a situation of conflict. You will have
decided who is to be your central figure, the one whose story it is.
You are in sympathy with this character (whom we will call X) and
your task is to engage the reader and make him care what happens.
Start your novel just before a big scene. It might not reach its peak
until the second chapter, or even the third, but the reader must be
drawn swiftly into the mainstream of the story and sense the
promise of important developments in store. Decide on the main
problem confronting X, the problem which will be with him
throughout the book, reaching some kind of climax – for better or
worse – in the last chapter. Don't introduce more than three or four
characters by name in Chapter One and don't confuse the reader
with too many facts or ideas.

The first paragraph is naturally of great importance. This is the
point at which you will captivate your reader or possibly lose him
for ever. Study the following openings. Some will attract you, some
may not, but they all have something to teach you about novel-
writing.

> Mother died today. Or, maybe, yesterday; I can't be sure. The
> telegram from the Home says: *Your mother passed away. Funeral
> tomorrow. Deep sympathy.* Which leaves the matter doubtful; it
> could have been yesterday.
>
> (*The Outsider* by Albert Camus)

> I had a fine Norton that year, in Bhowani. It's got smashed up since,
> but it was looking good the day I went down to see Victoria after she
> came back from the Army. I got to the house, cut off the engine, and

sat there in the saddle while it coughed, hiccuped once or twice, and died. The truth is I was afraid to go in. She'd been away a long time. She was an officer. She'd have changed.

(Bhowani Junction by John Masters)

A strange melancholy pervades me to which I hesitate to give the grave and beautiful name of sorrow. The idea of sorrow has always appealed to me, but now I am almost ashamed of its complete egoism. I have known boredom, regret, and occasionaly remorse, but never sorrow. Today it envelops me like a silken web, enervating and soft, and sets me apart from everybody else.

(Bonjour Tristesse by Françoise Sagan)

She walked down Fulham Broadway past a shop hung about with cheap underwear, the week-old baby clutched in her arms, his face brick red against his new white bonnet.

(Poor Cow by Nell Dunn)

Nobody could sleep. When morning came, assault craft would be lowered and a first wave of troops would ride through the surf and charge ashore on the beach at Anopopei. All over the ship, all through the convoy, there was a knowledge that in a few hours some of them were going to be dead.

(The Naked and the Dead by Norman Mailer)

On a bleak and gusty Saturday afternoon in March, the 2.45 bus from Market Square, Farbridge, arrived at the corner of Mayton Park Avenue, and stopped just long enough to allow a young woman carrying a portable typewriter to descend, which she did gracefully but grumpily. She was a small, dark and rather fierce young woman; and was wearing her old blue coat and felt hat, her old red dress that had never recovered from the cleaners, stockings that had laddered and not been too well repaired; and she was sure she was looking terrible, and did not care much, having no immediate joy in life. Her name was Laura Casey.

(Festival at Farbridge by J. B. Priestley)

Simpkins, alderman, ex-mayor of this town, engineer by trade, longtime widower in public, longtime lover of a married woman in private. (Simpkins was discreet, never gossiped about this relationship, and people were better at live-and-let-live than they sometimes got credit for.)

(A Raging Calm by Stan Barstow)

Everybody agreed with Mrs Baskett that her baby was a most remarkable child. They delighted to hear how, exploring the cellar, she ate coal to see how it tasted; how, investigating matches, she set the nursery curtains on fire and nearly burnt down the house. They admired the child's power of uproarious laughter at nothing at all; her shouts of rage, her egotism, her greed; and they went away and said that Tabitha Baskett was after all a very ordinary child, and rather a plain one. They shook their heads over the future of a plain girl with a mother so ill and feeble, a father so erratic.

(A Fearful Joy by Joyce Cary)

Afternoons seem unending on branch-line stations in England in summer time. The spiked shelter prints an unmoving shadow on the platform, geraniums blaze, whitewashed stones assault the eye. Such trains as come only add to the air of fantasy, to the idea of the scene being symbolic, or encountered at one level while suggesting another even more alienating.

(A Wreath of Roses by Elizabeth Taylor)

In 1928 my foot was hurting all the time, so they took it off and gave me an aluminium one that only hurt about three-quarters of the time. It would be all right for a bit, and then any one of about fifty things would start it off and it would give me hell.

(The Small Back Room by Nigel Balchin)

Lolita, light of my life, fire of my loins. My sin, my soul. Lo-lee-ta: the tip of the tongue taking a trip of three steps down the palate to tap, at three, on the teeth. Lo.Lee.Ta.

(Lolita by Vladimir Nabokov)

Read them again and marvel at the variety of styles, finding encouragement and inspiration in the immense range of possibilities open to you when you write your own first paragraph.

You may be in doubt as to the precise point in the life of X when you should begin. What age is he to be when the story opens? If something vital happened to him at the age of ten, should you begin the actual narrative on that day, or should you start later – perhaps when he is grown-up – and let the childhood incident be revealed in flashback? I should advise you to use the flashback technique with caution although it can be very effective. Sometimes the only way to solve this problem is to write and re-write until you find the answer by trial and error. No matter how carefully you have planned your opening on your 1–30 sheet of foolscap, you might well discover, when the actual writing begins, that you have to make some alterations.

The first chapter of my fourth novel, *The Flesh is Strong*, illustrates how I solved this problem myself.

The first humiliation came when I was seven. It was only a small incident at a Christmas party, long ago in 1938, but even now I can hardly bear to think of it. It marked a turning point in my life; until that moment I was not really aware of being ugly.

The party was at a much grander house than ours – the home of one of my mother's friends, at the other side of Leicester. There was a wide white staircase leading up to a high room with gold cupids round the cornice and when I walked into that room with my sister Dulcie, wearing my first party frock, I felt like a princess.

My father had bought me the dress specially for this occasion – a flamboyant, frilly affair with a tiered pink net skirt. My short wiry black hair was parted neatly at the side and held back with a pink slide studded with glass diamonds. It was a tawdry little slide but I had admired it in a shop window and my father had gone straight in and bought it for me. He was like that. He would never say, "Shall I buy it for you?"; that might lead to hesitations and reservations which could cloud or destroy the whole impulse. So long as there was a pound or two in his pocket – and there wasn't usually much more – he was ready to spend it on anyone who wanted anything.

He was a mountain of a man, black-haired, black-moustached, with a big nose and heavy jaw, like mine. His ears and nostrils sprouted black hairs as thick as wire but his eyes were babyish – like little brown velvet buttons. He had a low, slow voice and a laugh that shook the floorboards. I called him Poppo.

In the party room a glittering Christmas tree stood in front of a tall mirror so that at first I thought there were two trees. About twenty children were sitting on the floor waiting for a film show to start. My sister and I sat down among them on the thick, plum-red carpet. Dulcie was two years older than I. She was delicately built, with long auburn hair, and she looked very beautiful in a white dress sewn with silver sequins.

I said to her, "I thought there were two Christmas trees at first. It looks like it, doesn't it?"

She frowned. "Why should there be two trees?"

"I said I *thought* there were two, because of the looking-glass."

"How silly!"

"I don't think it's silly."

"It is silly. It's *silly*!"

I turned away to a boy who sat, cross-legged, on the other side of me. He was about my own age, with curly black hair and a pale serious face. I wanted to talk to him, but he looked so remote with his big dreamy black eyes fixed on the tree, that I decided against it. When the show began – a dull Nature Film about otters – I studied him in the flash and glimmer of the screen and became so excitedly aware of his dark, still presence that when the lights went up I dared not look at him but turned to Dulcie.

"Did you like it?" I asked her.

"No, I didn't. I thought it was silly. I want to *play* something."
She tossed her hair and stood up, smoothing out her frock.

All the children got up as some kind of game was announced and
the boy stood near me with his hands in his pockets. I was trying to
summon the courage to speak to him when I felt a cold hand on my
arm and I looked up into the thin face of a woman with dangling
black earrings, mother's friend, whose home it was. She smiled at me
and extended her other hand to clutch at the shoulder of the boy.

"Now, Florence," she said, drawing the two of us together,
"this is Nigel." She had a lilting, talking-down-to-children kind of
voice. "You two will be partners for our next game and Nigel will
look after you, won't you, Nigel?"

I glanced at him, my cheeks burning with pleasure, but as he
stared into my face, his great eyes were dark with affront. "No!" he
cried. "I don't want to play with *her* – she's *ugly*!"

It happened nearly thirty years ago but I can still hear his voice,
still see the proud tilt of his averted head as he rejected me. The lady
chided him in a horrified undertone and hustled him away. I was left
with Dulcie and I looked at her helplessly, my eyes filling with tears.
She studied me carefully for a few moments, gave a simpering little
laugh, and turned away.

The lights of the Christmas tree fused together in splintered
blobs of tears and I raced out of the room and hid behind a grand-
father's clock in a deserted alcove. The powerful ticking shook
against my shoulder as I huddled in the narrow, dusty space between
the clock and the wall, and it comforted me like the nearness of some
great benevolent animal. I crouched there for a while, the tears
running down into my mouth, and suddenly the clock began to
wheeze and whirr, an elaborate prelude to chiming the hour. I was
just going to scramble out when I heard two women talking on the
landing nearby. Their voices were only audible between the chimes,
blotted out by each reverberating stroke, but as the sixth and final
echo died away, their conversation occupied my whole attention.

"I could have *murdered* Nigel!" It was the sing-song voice of the
lady with the earrings. "Children are so cruel. They say exactly what
they think. But that younger Matthews girl really is *grotesque*. Fancy
dressing a great creature like that in pink net! I ask you! Have you
seen her? Do you know the one I mean?"

"Florence Matthews – oh, yes, I know. A tragedy, isn't it? Her
sister Dulcie is so pretty, too. Quite exquisite, in fact. Makes you
wonder what the dear Lord is up to sometimes."

"It really does. Well, I must away to dish out the presents from the tree. Isn't Christmas *hell*!"

I scrubbed my sticky face with a wet handkerchief, gulping against the sobs. The footsteps retreated along the landing and I heard a door open and close, letting out a momentary babble from the party. I dreaded going back but there was still an hour to go before Mother came to collect us. Besides, I wanted my present.

When I opened the door the tall lady came weaving and smiling across the room to welcome me. "Florence, my *dear*, we wondered where ever you'd got to. Come along; you're just in time for the presents." The cold hand was on my arm again and, as I accompanied her to the tree, I remembered that same voice on the landing: "*grotesque*", she had called me. I had no idea what it meant; I would have to ask Poppo.

She gave me an oblong box wrapped in holly-patterned paper but I was hardly aware of it. I had just caught sight of Nigel and Dulcie laughing together in a corner. I was certain they were laughing at me.

I did not realise then, at the age of seven, the enormity of the hurt that had been done to me, but that was the day that marked the indelible branding of myself as unacceptable to the opposite sex. I had been born an ugly girl, with the kind of structural defects that can never change. I was thick and graceless from the inmost bone, body and face alike, the victim, it seemed, of a cruel trick. An ugly girl is a contradiction in terms, a perversion. Girls are pretty things, designed for adoration; a girl without beauty is like a bird without wings – a creature denied its natural element.

That is the end of Chapter One. Chapter Two begins:

It was not until I met Gregory, twenty years later, that the real pain began.

On a wet April evening in 1958 Dulcie and I went up to London from Guildford to see an Italian film . . .

I had originally started the book quite differently, beginning when Florence was twenty-seven and writing in the third person. After months of difficult progress and unsuccessful revision I had to begin again. I decided to reframe it in the first person and to open the book in 1938, showing the scene with Nigel in immediate narrative instead of in retrospect. As soon as I started work on this new approach I felt it was going to be all right.

I would advise this method of avoiding flashback to any writer with a similar problem, *but only if the early scene is strong enough and important enough to warrant it.*

I have always found it necessary to arrange some kind of

confrontation in the first chapter. It might take place between X and another person or persons; it might be that X is on the brink of some vital decision. Whatever it is it must be closely concerned with the theme of your novel. Here we see the essential relationship between Theme and Plot. Never start with a situation, however interesting in itself, which is not deeply relevant to the novel as a whole. And avoid misleading the reader by commencing your book in a manner which is not typical of the rest of it.

Don't be alarmed if the beginning seems particularly difficult to write. You are getting to know your characters by hearing them speak and seeing them in action. It is bound to take time. Once you are launched and have reached a better understanding of your characters, you will find you can work more quickly and easily. Don't try to hurry the beginning; it's like building a hasty foundation for a house. In the long run you don't save time at all because the house collapses and has to be rebuilt.

Avoid involving your readers in long detailed explanations and descriptions. This applies at all stages of the novel, but most particularly in Chapter One. This is the chapter which seems to demand a great deal of exposition and yet it is the one, above all others, in which you must avoid boring your reader. Get the story moving at the outset and introduce your explanations gradually and in small doses, interwoven with action and dialogue. Your handling of this problem will obviously depend on the kind of book you are writing; a crisp suspense story would allow less description than a slower-moving novel where atmosphere and character are all-important.

Watch the ending of this first chapter; be careful not to give away too much. Choose a moment when you have come to the end of a phase, but when the tension is still unresolved.

Start writing, and continue to work regularly, however vaguely you see your way and however discouraged you feel. If you write *something* you will find that eventually the story will develop. You can then keep going back and re-writing in the light of the new discoveries you make about your characters and plot. In any case you will probably need to re-write the first chapter when the whole book is finished. This is an enjoyable task to keep in mind, something to look forward to as you build up your novel, page by page.

9

Plot

"As regards plot I find real life no help at all. Real life seems to have
no plots. And as I think a plot desirable and almost necessary, I have
this extra grudge against life."
Ivy Compton-Burnett

Plot grows out of characterisation and conflict. If your
protagonist is faced with some major problem at the outset, if he
desperately wants something which is difficult to obtain (and this is
the basic story line of most novels), his devious strivings towards
this end, together with the failures and successes which ensue, will
form the composition of your plot. You will need to drive your
main characters to their limits if we are to see what they are really
made of, and the resulting tensions will lead to the development of
a strong story. When Isak Dinesen was interviewed for *The Paris
Review* she said: "*I start with a tingle, a kind of feeling of the story
I will write. Then come the characters, and they take over, they
make the story. All this ends by being a plot.*" That is exactly the
way I work myself.

Try to keep your characters in some kind of intriguing
situation from which they will move into a new and even more
intriguing situation. It could be a state of physical danger, or
something as intangible as the fear of a dream, but there should
always be some kind of dilemma, some knife-edge of drama close
at hand, even if it is only a delusion in the mind of a character.

Plot is really a question of one thing leading to another. For
me, as the action develops, it is rather like crossing a wide shallow
river on a series of stepping-stones. The far bank is the ending,
dimly perceived, but the present moment is the stone upon which I
am standing. The fast-moving stream is around me, but here I am,
on this one stone, in this one scene. Out of the corner of my eye I
can see the next stone, and I am preparing to take a further leap.

Take the example of my novel *The Flesh is Strong*. In the train
back to Guildford, Florence and her sister Dulcie meet the engaging
Gregory who is in the same compartment. I had no idea, when I
began that chapter, that there was going to be a derailment, but as I
wrote I became aware that the train would begin to lurch and sway
and that an accident was inevitable; the drama of the crash was

bound up with the emotional involvement of the three characters. That's the way it goes . . . But of course you are constantly retracing your steps to amend earlier passages in the light of new developments. That's where we have to part company with the stepping-stones analogy; when you are crossing a river you don't keep going back. But isn't that a cardinal difference between fiction and reality? In real life we can't go back to alter things (if only we could!), and fiction can appear more "true" than reality itself, because it is devised to illustrate the truth in the light of greater knowledge and deeper understanding.

In *Aspects of the Novel*, E. M. Forster has this to say:

> *"Let us define plot. We have defined a story as a narrative of events arranged in their time-sequence. A plot is also a narrative of events, the emphasis falling on causality. 'The king died and then the queen died,' is a story. 'The king died, and then the queen died of grief,' is a plot. The time-sequence is preserved, but the sense of causality overshadows it. Or again: 'The queen died, no one knew why, until it was discovered that it was through grief at the death of the king.' This is a plot with a mystery in it, a form capable of high development . . . a plot demands intelligence and memory also."*

This sets me thinking, Aha, but was it *really* grief that caused her death? Perhaps it was; perhaps she had loved the king so deeply that she could not live without him and died of a broken heart. And that would imply a certain weakness of character. But perhaps it wasn't grief. Perhaps she died of remorse because she had treated him so badly. Perhaps it was self-pity that killed her. Or terror at the prospect of facing her royal responsibilities alone. Or maybe she was murdered . . . This is the way we think when we analyse our characters in depth in order to develop the narrative. The answers to similar questions in relation to your particular "queen", the one you have created, will determine the way in which your plot unfolds.

If you have an idea for a dramatic episode that might occur later in your book, and you feel like writing it up while it is fresh in your imagination, it is rewarding and satisfying to do so. Nevertheless, you should bear in mind that your whole concept of that episode will probably have changed when the time comes to insert it. Never shrink from the hard work involved in re-writing. You can so easily ruin a book by "making do" with something which you know, in your heart of hearts, is a lazy second-best.

It is a common fault with beginners to describe an event in retrospect, or in conversation, or in somebody's memory, when it ought to be shown as a scene in direct narrative.

Take this example of a personal experience in real life:

a) You read about a car crash in a newspaper. It doesn't mean very much to you.
b) Somebody tells you about an accident he has seen. This means a little more.
c) You actually witness the accident. More still.
d) You yourself are *involved* in the accident.

If you can identify with your characters and involve them directly, you will foster that quality of immediacy which makes the reader feel as if he is living in your book and can hardly bear to put it down. On my desk I have a card which says "*Make a Scene of it!*" and I advise you to bear this phrase in mind whenever you sit down to write.

Finally, a word about contrived plots. What are they and how can they be recognised and avoided?

If you find yourself thinking, What can I make them do now? you are on dangerous ground. The proper question is surely, "What *are* they doing now?" The action should grow naturally and inevitably from a steady build-up of characterisation and deeply-felt motivation. You are watching the story unfold, even as you devise it. The characters and situations for a novel can be chosen by the spin of a plot-machine wheel (lion-tamer meets air-hostess in a Siberian salt-mine), or they can evolve from the writer's obsessive preoccupation with some personal problem. Between these two extremes, there are endless variations. A newspaper item can trigger off a fine novel, but only if the novelist is already deeply concerned about that particular aspect of human relationships. If he merely says to himself, with no sense of compassion or involvement, "There might be a novel in that," the resulting book would be "contrived", even though a skilled writer could present it in a way that would appeal to many readers. I am writing here about my own particular aims and ideals with regard to the "straight" novel and I agree with Arthur Miller that "*a writer should speak from the genuine centre of his soul*". If he does this, he will never permit himself to devise a contrived plot. If he is tempted towards it, he will recognise it as such, and discard it.

Plot, for many beginners, is a difficult problem, but if you care deeply about your theme, know your characters, and work from scene to scene, you will find the action unfolding more readily than you would have believed possible.

10

Construction

"The most important thing in a work of art is that it should have a kind of focus, i.e. there should be some place where all the rays meet or from which they issue."

Leo Tolstoy

The shape of a novel can be likened to a tree. The backbone of your story is the trunk, reaching its climax in the topmost branches. The side branches are the sub-plots, and the shape is unbalanced if one of them becomes too long or too thick. Twigs, leaves and fruits are the details that give light, shade, colour, and a variety of textures and moods. You can extend the analogy by seeing the theme of the novel as the roots of the tree, sensed but unseen, and giving sustenance to the whole creation. Your fertile imagination is the rich soil that nurtured the seed in the first place.

For me, this image illustrates the essentials of a novel: gradual growth, stability and power, delicacy, beauty, sadness and gaiety. It is deeply-rooted, yet free; sturdy, yet resilient; always changing, while retaining its own distinction. Keep these qualities in mind, particularly the strength of the backbone, the trunk. If one of your branches seems to be growing too strongly, you must either prune it, or decide that it deserves to take the place of the trunk. In this case you will have a good deal of re-thinking to do; you might even have to grow a new tree.

Relevance

In life, everything is relevant; not so in the novel. As Alfred Hitchcock once said: *"Drama is like real life with the dull bits cut out."* You must focus, emphasise and eliminate, moulding the story into a satisfying whole without one extraneous word. Don't allow yourself to be side-tracked by bewitching possibilities that have nothing to do with *this* novel. There will be other novels. *Selection* is a word that should be constantly in your mind. *"If we do not wish to select,"* wrote Moravia, *"then ten thousand pages will not be enough to describe even a room."* (*Man as an End*)

Beware of the temptation to include a piece of description, an episode, or a conversation, just because it has for you a strong personal significance. You have probably laboured over the writing

43

of it with intense and loving care, but sadly enough, these are often the very passages that must be discarded. They have no real place in the novel; they are merely exercises for our private delight and it is a sign of our professionalism when we recognise that the structure of the novel would be damaged if they were allowed to remain.

Another vital aspect of construction is the danger of airing one's own personal views, of preaching or moralising. Just tell the truth about your characters and their activities, as far as possible without judging them, and avoid the temptation of trying to convert the reader. Your attitude to life will emerge between the lines, without any effort on your part. Let this suffice. A novel is not primarily a political, social or religious document; it is a *story*, and it is meant to entertain. If it is a good novel it will help people to understand one another because it will be written with compassion and insight, but any deliberate attempt to impose your opinions will mar the shape of your book and reduce its artistic merit.

Balance

When you write a novel you can either shoot the rapids or paddle gently downstream in calm waters, but no novel should be all rapids or all calm waters. The crises and lulls must be carefully balanced, although your own temperament will dictate the pace of the story. In any case, there should be increasingly strong tensions as the book progresses. Never let a novel "tail off" towards the end. Many novels give the impression of a tired author, dozing fitfully over the final chapters, as if he has lost interest in the fate of his characters and only wants to be rid of them. On the other hand, there is sometimes a sense of careless haste towards the end, as if the novelist was in a tearing hurry to finish the book, pocket his advance, and fly off to the Bahamas!

Your novel must carry the reader steadily and strongly through a variety of moods, providing peaks of drama with calmer spells between. The lulls, however, must always lead inexorably towards new dramas, and even the moments of greatest serenity should carry the promise of important and unknown developments. Always give the reader a little more than he expects, never less; give him, too, if you can, a feast of happenings he could never have dreamed of, but which, when they come, are entirely acceptable and convincing.

Dramatising a Situation

First of all, make sure that the situation you have in mind is credible and that it is vital to this novel. Then, having decided at what point in the narrative the particular situation is to occur, lead up to it with care, creating the right atmosphere and mood. The situation might be completely unexpected but it will be convincing if you have prepared the way for it. The leading-up paragraphs, although less dramatic in themselves, make the moments of drama more telling and significant, not only by contrast, but because you are subtly building up the tension; the reader senses the approach of the storm in the stillness that precedes it.

Sometimes the preparation for a dramatic situation might begin a dozen chapters earlier – or even on the first page of the novel. Death is more tragic if the person who dies was deeply loved; joy is more intense after despair; betrayal more terrible after perfect trust . . . Seize every chance for added drama, so long as everything is relevant and has, for you, the ring of truth. Make a conscious effort to intrigue and excite the reader so that your own involvement is transmitted to him and he is moved as you are moved.

Careful timing is vital. Extend the build-up long enough to tantalise but not long enough to bore. When you reach the situation itself, make sure that you are inside the mind of your viewpoint character and try to see it and experience it as vividly as your character does. Make a scene of it from the one character's angle and don't be afraid of driving him to the limit of his endurance, even though you might well be driving yourself along with him! Nevertheless, you must always beware of overplaying the possibilities; feel it all yourself, but select with care the aspects to be stated and those to be left unwritten but implicit. It is perhaps this constant labour of selection which acts as a steadying influence and helps the compulsive novelist to remain (comparatively) sane.

Suspense

The mastery of suspense is not only vital in a thriller; it is vital in every story, however leisurely. There must always be a desire on the part of the reader to follow the lives of your characters to the very last chapter. If the novel is a good one, he will reach the end with a sigh of regret. He will also feel stimulated and in some way satisfied, even though the outcome may be far from happy. Every novel needs a strong ending, even if it is the "slice of life" kind of book that leaves many questions unsolved. You must satisfy the reader, yet also leave him wondering how the characters are making out in that mysterious world that lies beyond the final page.

The story must be gradually unravelled, each paragraph

leading fluently from the one before. Avoid large leaps in time or space, except between chapters. A novice once began a paragraph in the middle of a chapter with: "Ten years later he emigrated to Australia."

Keep the time sequences well-balanced throughout the book. For instance, it would be a mistake to construct the first three-quarters of your novel to cover one eventful month, and then allow jumps of two or three years between each chapter in the last quarter of the book. On the other hand, you could easily set the first half in 1955, have a leap of twenty years, and continue the second half in 1975. In such a case, you might choose to divide your novel into Parts I and II.

Make the time and place clear beyond doubt at the beginning of every chapter. Bear in mind that you, as the author, know exactly when and where the action occurs, but the reader knows only what you tell him. However, avoid over-clarification; *always credit your reader with a degree of intelligence no less than your own.*

When you introduce your characters, reveal their more obvious attributes at the outset. I was once astonished to discover, nearly halfway through a novel by an amateur, that a man I had imagined as blond and clean shaven had a bushy black beard. Another young writer had deliberately withheld from the reader the valuable information that her heroine was blind, although the other characters must have known all the time. If the "viewpoint" character knows something to be true, then this information must not be concealed in order to create a "surprise" later. This technique is often used by beginners; they have no idea that they are cheating. In his book *Aspects of the Novel*, E. M. Forster writes: "*Every action or word in a plot ought to count; it ought to be economical and spare; even when complicated it should be organic and free from dead matter, it may be difficult or easy, it may and should contain mysteries, but it ought not to mislead.*"

As far as possible introduce your description along with your narrative. E.g. "As she put on her frayed cotton gloves he noticed that her wrists were scored with red scratches. Perhaps she had a cat at home, a cat with a temper." The reader will wonder how she got them, and the reason, of course, must be vital to the story. Most probably it won't be the cat!

The Ending

How do you know when the time has come to conclude your story? Think back to that initial question: "What am I trying to say?" Have you said it? Have you told your story, rounded it off, resolved – to some degree at least – the problem that bedevilled your main character? Have you finished with that section of his life which relates to your theme? If so, it is time to prepare the final pages. Isak Dinesen again: *"A proper tale has a shape and an outline. In a painting the frame is important. Where does the picture end? What details should one include? Or omit! Where does the line go that cuts off the picture?"* In an interview for *The Paris Review* John Updike had this to say: *"In the execution there has to be a 'happiness' that can't be willed or fore-ordained. It has to sing, click, something. I try instantly to set in motion a certain forward tilt of suspense or curiosity, and at the end of the story or novel to rectify the tilt, to complete the motion."*

I dislike the conventional "happy ending" with all the pink bows neatly tied, but I think the reader should feel there is the hope of something better in the future and that the main character has gained something of value from his experiences. Nevertheless, many fine novels end on a note of despair; the outcome must depend on the writer's attitude to his theme and to his characters.

When you are near the end of your book, you can probably improve the shape by reading it through from the beginning with great care, noting any loose ends or superfluous passages. This process is rather like lacing a tall boot; before tying the final knot, you pull all the laces tightly together, right from the bottom.

Nothing but experience can teach you the art of construction, but it can be summarised in the one word *form*. A book can be ragged, lop-sided, jumpy, muddled and dull. Or it can be compact, shapely, streamlined, clear and readable. If you have the talent and understand the basic principles, you only need time and determination to produce a well constructed novel.

11

Style

"I know of only one rule: style cannot be too *clear*, too *simple* . . ."
Stendhal

Your style is you, unique as your fingerprints. It grows naturally from the practice of your craft; it cannot and must not be deliberate. Nevertheless, you must work to eliminate such errors as faulty grammar, repetition, clichés and clumsy sentences. It is experience alone which can teach you to write with simplicity and clarity and to discard some of your best-loved paragraphs because they are overwritten or irrelevant.

Perhaps the greatest problem for the beginner is that of preserving spontaneity. How is one to prune and shape one's work without losing that first vitality which is so precious and delightful? I think this is the measure of a novelist's artistry – the extent to which he can strike the balance between freedom and control, richness and simplicity. My advice is to write fully in the first instance, returning later to cut away the superfluous material with ruthless determination. Never allow a "purple passage" to remain. This, as you may know, is the name often given to flowery descriptions in which the writer has indulged in clichés, sentimentality, an abundance of adjectives and possibly a hackneyed situation for good measure. To quote a published example might be unwise but you probably know exactly where to look for one!

Interviewed for *Paris Match*, Georges Simenon said: "*Just one piece of general advice from a writer has been very useful to me. It was from Colette. I was writing short stories for* Le Matin, *and Colette was literary editor at that time. I remember I gave her two short stories and she returned them and I tried again and tried again. Finally she said, 'Look, it is too literary, always too literary.' So I followed her advice. It's what I do when I write, the main job when I re-write.*" The interviewer then asked Simenon: "*What do you mean by 'too literary'? What do you cut out, certain kinds of words?*" Simenon replied: "*Adjectives, adverbs, and every word which is there just to make an effect. Every sentence which is there just for the sentence . . .*"

For years I have followed the maxim: "If in doubt, leave it

out!'' Always state a little less than you feel is necessary, rather than more. To state less is not only a useful restraint for the writer; it is also an inspiration to the reader because it leaves him free to add his own contribution. Reading a good novel is an extremely creative pursuit.

It is helpful for the novice to take a random page of his recent work and go through it carefully, sentence by sentence, searching for words and phrases which could be deleted without altering the meaning or sacrificing anything of vital significance. It is almost certain that any page of amateur prose, however talented the writer, can be improved by cutting – sometimes by as much as twenty-five per cent.

There is a well-known slogan: ''Never use a long word when a short one would do.'' I agree. But I would add this rider: ''Never use a short word when a long one would be better.'' ''*Proper words in proper places*'' was Swift's definition of good style.

Try to find an unusual way of expressing your meaning in order to make it memorable, but the unusual can also be simple. The following examples illustrate this point:

> The darkness outside the open door suddenly drew back and for a moment they could see the palm trees bending in a strange yellow light the colour of old photographs.
>
> (*A Burnt-Out Case* by Graham Greene)

> Lime trees were coming to life by the laneside, tiny erectile buds emerging to enjoy the spring and shining like emeralds, fresh enough to quench one's thirst.
>
> (*Saturday Night and Sunday Morning* by Alan Sillitoe)

> On a footbridge between an island and the mainland a man and woman stood talking, leaning on the rail. In the intense cold, which made everyone hurry, they had chosen to make this long summerlike pause. Their oblivious stillness made them look like lovers – actually, their elbows were some inches apart; they were riveted not to each other but to what she said. Their thick coats made their figures sexless and stiff as chessmen: they were well-to-do, inside bulwarks of fur and cloth their bodies generated a steady warmth; they could only see the cold – or, if they felt it, they only felt it at their extremities. Now and then he stamped on the bridge, or she brought her muff up to her face. Ice pushed down the channel under the bridge, so that while they talked their reflections were constantly broken up.
>
> (*The Death of the Heart* by Elizabeth Bowen)

Be sure that your writing is consistent throughout the novel and that you have chosen a style which is your own; it is a great mistake to imitate another author, although we are bound to absorb the subtle influences of those we admire. It might be unwise to read too many novels while you are engaged on writing one.

What about humour? Yes, of course you should introduce it – but only if it comes naturally. It is useless to "try to be funny" in a novel; humour emerges from the situation and unless you feel the stirrings of an inward chuckle, write it straight.

There is a certain practice known as "author talking" which entails giving your own personal view of things as you tell the story and reminding the reader of your presence. The prime example in the old days was "Dear Reader". You may find instances of "author talking" in first-class modern novels but I have never cared for it because it destroys the illusion of reality. I agree with Angus Wilson when he says: *"All fiction for me is a kind of magic and trickery – a confidence trick, trying to make people believe something is true that isn't."* When the author intrudes, that magic dies.

If you're anything like me, you probably skipped the introduction, but I suggested that a writer can afford to ignore the guidelines only when he attains a mastery of his craft. I think the same applies to other arts; the laws of counterpoint and perspective should be understood before they are broken, so that any deviations can be knowingly designed to produce a more telling piece of work.

Take this extract from Margaret Drabble's *The Realms of Gold*:

> They drove through the suburban countryside, through the pine woods and the bracken, as the colour deepened. It was pink and silver, russet and coral, the silver birches pink in the faint premonition of a sunset, the bark of the pine trees darkening to a wilder Scots redness, a few leaves of last year pink and copper, but above all the bracken, the dead bracken, with its lovely, special, eccentric cold burnished leafy metallic dead but promising beauty.

In context I found these adjectives arresting and delightful, but if a beginner in my Creative Writing class used nine in a row, I should certainly protest. Which all goes to show that there are no inflexible rules. Perhaps the only valid ones are those you eventually make for yourself. If you make them in the light of knowledge and experience, you will write your novel in your own original way, confident that it is the right way for you.

Avoid generalisation, as far as possible. If you say that a magazine lay on the table, let us know if it was a brand new glossy one or a tatty, dog-eared copy with the cover missing. Words like "lovely", "pretty", "interesting" and "ordinary" have little meaning. Don't say "It was a lovely day"; say in what *way* it was lovely. Don't say a girl was pretty; describe her as someone quite different from any other pretty girl we have seen or read about. And never say a person looked ordinary; there are a thousand ways of looking ordinary. In any case, to a novelist there is no such thing as an ordinary person.

This, perhaps, is the secret of good style – a way of writing that tells the truth about life in terms that your readers can recognise and appreciate. *"To write well,"* said Aristotle, *"express yourself like the common people but think like a wise man."*

12

The Mechanics of Improvement
"Teach yourself by your own mistakes; people learn only by error."
William Faulkner

I think you must be prepared to write a bad, unpublishable novel – perhaps more than one – in order to learn your craft. Many amateurs expect success after a few months of haphazard work without professional advice. They are bound to be disappointed. No pianist would expect to give a public concert after only a few months of practice, but writers sometimes dream of getting a book published with hardly any apprenticeship at all. It may happen to one in ten thousand, but there is no quick way to success, and anyone who is not prepared for sustained hard work should give up the idea of publishing a novel.

The length of time you spend on revision will depend, of course, on how carefully you wrote the first draft. Some writers like to finish the whole book before polishing, others have to perfect each chapter as far as possible before going on to the next. I belong to the latter school, but in spite of this, there is still plenty of re-writing to be done after the first draft is completed. I write in longhand first, making alterations as I go along. When the first chapter is done I can hardly read it; there are dozens of deletions, tightly crammed insertions, arrows pointing to scrawls up the sides of the page, asterisks and ringed asterisks marking more additions, sometimes on separate sheets of paper. Some novelists think it all out beforehand, and their first draft is as neat as a school essay. Of course it doesn't matter in the least which way you work, so long as the end result is all it should be.

The next step, for me, is to type out the chaotic scribble so that I can see what I have written. In the process of typing I make many more alterations. I always take a carbon copy, because I send out my final draft for professional typing, and it is unthinkable to lose sight of a one-and-only manuscript.

When I have written and roughly typed out the whole novel, I read it through from the beginning, making any necessary alterations. This is what I call the second draft. Some of the lesser amendments can be written on the typescript (provided they are neat enough for my typist to understand) but it is often necessary to retype whole pages. To save renumbering, it is quite in order to number additional sheets 49a, 49b, etc.

See what Robert Graves had to say about revision in an interview on BBC Television: *"Everything goes through a great many drafts. With prose about three or four . . . then it goes to be typed after which I can see it again clearly. Then it goes through another stage here, and later gets knocked about again, and after that it settles down . . . It is the greatest fun making things as easy as possible for the reader while keeping the sense and integrity of what you are writing."*

Most serious writers, I think, work this way. Joyce Cary said: *"I re-write a great deal and I work over the whole book and cut out anything that does not belong to the emotional development, the texture of feeling."* Isak Dinesen was asked if she re-wrote her tales very much. *"Oh, I do, I do,"* she said. *"It's hellish. Over and over again. Then when I think I'm finished, and Clara copies them out to send to the publishers, I look over them, and have a fit, and re-write again."*

The following points might be useful when you revise your first draft:

1) Cut out superfluous matter. This can mean anything from the elimination of single words – often adjectives – to whole sentences and scenes. Watch out for repetition, irrelevance, flowery descriptions and "soap-box" passages. Reading onto tape will often reveal faults you had overlooked.

2) Expand where necessary to give more substance and clarity. Add subtle pointers to herald approaching crises in such a way that these remain unexpected but are wholly acceptable when they occur. (E.g. If a woman is later to rescue a child from drowning in a rough sea, let us know in advance that she is a strong swimmer – or at least that she is an athletic kind of person.) Write in bridging paragraphs to avoid uneasy transitions from one passage to the next.

3) Check clarity of time and place, sometimes rearranging scenes – or even whole chapters – to make quite certain that the reader knows when and where the action occurs. I usually scribble a pencilled note at the beginning of each chapter to say when the action takes place; this helps me to keep track of the narrative and also reminds me to consider what the subsidiary characters are doing.

4) Make sure the endings of the chapters are suspenseful and yet

53

complete. A chapter ending often needs a further sentence to round it off; on the other hand, it might require curtailment in order to reserve some intriguing development for the following chapter.

5) Check all facts with great care. It might be the distance between Rome and Naples, lighting-up time in New York on Christmas Day or the look of the foyer at the London Palladium, but if your novel is concerned with established and unalterable facts they *must* be correct.

6) Check punctuation, paying special attention to superfluous commas and exclamation marks. If you are in doubt about the correct use of colons and semicolons consult Fowler's *Modern English Usage* or Strunk and White's *Elements of Style* and study the work of good contemporary novelists.

Apart from the points mentioned above, a number of elusive faults may bother you when you read your novel from beginning to end. If you have a feeling, however slight, that something is amiss, never let it pass. A trusted fellow writer might help – a fresh eye can often locate the trouble. Or a few days' rest could restore the critical vision you need.

A third and fourth draft will sometimes be necessary; whatever happens, make sure you have done your utmost before you submit your novel to a publisher. Many a good writer has thrown away the chance of getting his first book into print for the sake of an extra month or two of work. The reason might be exhaustion, laziness, impatience, over-confidence or the need for ready cash, but I do entreat you not to make this mistake.

13

A Page Dissected

"I have in mind another human being who will understand me. I count on this."

Saul Bellow

I think it might be helpful if I go through the first page of my novel *The Flesh is Strong* (reproduced in Chapter Eight) and analyse in detail my reasons for writing as I did. There will be no need to refer back; I shall quote a paragraph at a time and follow each with an explanation.

"*The first humiliation came when I was seven. It was only a small incident at a Christmas party, long ago in 1938, but even now I can hardly bear to think of it. It marked a turning point in my life; until that moment I was not really aware of being ugly.*"

This states the theme of the novel: the importance of a woman's looks in her relationships with the opposite sex. I had the idea for this book when I was in the Air Force. In 1944 I was posted to the Middle East and there was a girl in my billet who had no boy-friends because she was so ugly. She was a delightful person but she never had the chance of any fun. While the rest of us dolled ourselves up and went off to dances in Cairo she stayed indoors and read a book or wrote to her parents. It was so unjust; the pretty girls, however selfish or unkind, were surrounded by dashing young men in glamorous uniforms; the plain ones were left alone. That was when the idea first came to me although I didn't begin to write the book until twenty years later. By that time I was losing my own looks, which meant that the theme had acquired a deeper significance. This, perhaps, was why I returned to it at that particular time.

I chose as my main character a girl called Florence Matthews who was born with the kind of structural ugliness which does not change. She bore no resemblance to the girl in Cairo, nor to anyone else, so far as I know. I think I decided on her father's appearance first and made her resemble him. She is warm-hearted and passionate, an ideal lover except for her lack of beauty.

The first sentence is designed to engage the reader's interest from the outset; what can this humiliation be? People are always interested in each other's humiliations, whether in a kindly way or otherwise. The Christmas party was a paradox; the incident which hurt Florence so deeply was tragically alien to the spirit of Christmas. Nevertheless, I must admit that I didn't choose a Christmas party for this reason. It just came into my mind – the tree reflected in the mirror, the seven-year-old Florence in her pink party dress – and it is only now, faced with the task of analysis, that I realise I wrote better than I knew. This often happens to a writer; it is one of those rare, mystical bonuses that help to compensate for all the months of hard work. *"Long ago in 1938."* Why 1938? I was writing the book in 1964 and I wanted Florence to be in her early thirties at that time so that, as the narrator, she could tell the story of her unhappy love affair soon after it was over. The statement that *"even now I can hardly bear to think of it"* adds to the drama and encourages the reader to continue.

In this first paragraph I have not disclosed the sex of the main character. If I had the chance to revise that opening, I think I should make it clear at the very beginning, even though the reader tends to assume that a first-person narrator is of the same sex as the author. If he had imagined a boy, he would have had to do a quick re-think when he read the second paragraph. (This analysis is a valuable exercise for me; it reveals both faults and accidental virtues.)

"The party was at a much grander house that ours – the home of one of my mother's friends, at the other side of Leicester. There was a wide white staircase leading up to a high room with gold cupids round the cornice and when I walked into that room with my sister Dulcie, wearing my first party frock, I felt like a princess."

"A much grander house than ours." This gives a rough idea of Florence's social background and it also sets the scene for a dazzling occasion in her young mind, with the *"wide white staircase"* and *"gold cupids"*. In this way the humiliation, when it comes, is even more tragic. As novelists we must not hesitate to dramatise, however painful it may be.

"The house of one of my mother's friends." We now know that she has a mother and that the mother has well-to-do friends. I chose Leicester because I had only visited it for a short period and it still had a strangeness and fascination for me. Places you know only slightly can often provide better backgrounds than familiar ones.

"When I walked into that room with my sister Dulcie . . ."
Dulcie is a very important character in the story. When I first wrote this chapter I had introduced a different child, a friend, but this was a mistake. Whenever you can narrow down the field, focusing on a few characters and eliminating those who have no vital role to play, then do so. Dulcie is Florence's only sister, cold and selfish and outstandingly pretty. By introducing her here, as a child, I was able to give a foretaste of the anguish in store for Florence.

I am myself an only child so I had to imagine the relationship between sisters. My own mother was good-looking but unsympathetic. Her sister was plain but generous and understanding. And now I am learning things as I write. Florence, I suddenly realise, is based in appearance on this beloved aunt – the straight black hair and heavy jaw were hers exactly. I had not known it until this moment. (Novelists, analyse your books; you will learn a great deal about yourselves.)

"First party frock . . . felt like a princess." Here I added excitement and joy to render the approaching anguish more telling, but it wasn't done quite as deliberately as that implies. I felt for her; I *was* her; she was proud and self-assured – perhaps for the last time in her life.

"My father had bought me the dress specially for this occasion – a flamboyant, frilly affair with a tiered pink net skirt. My short wiry black hair was parted neatly at the side and held back with a pink slide studded with glass diamonds. It was a tawdry little slide but I had admired it in a shop window and my father had gone straight in and bought it for me. He was like that. He would never say, 'Shall I buy it for you?'; that might lead to hesitations and reservations which could cloud or destroy the whole impulse. So long as there was a pound or two in his pocket – and there wasn't usually much more – he was ready to spend it on anyone who wanted anything."

Florence's father is another key character and I wanted to show very clearly that a marvellous relationship existed between them. He bought her the dress and the slide. He was generous. And he was poor. I haven't indicated the reason for his poverty but that can wait. In any case it wasn't important to Florence at that time. I have suggested a divergence between Florence's mother, with her well-to-do friends, and her father with seldom more than a pound or two in his pocket. Florence's reference to the "flamboyant" dress and "tawdry" slide shows that she is now a person of some taste. And she obviously appreciates her father's impulsive generosity in never saying, "Shall I buy it for you?"

"My short wiry black hair . . ." It is always a problem, when you are writing in the first person, to indicate the main character's appearance; sometimes there seems to be no alternative to a mirror or a dark window or someone else's remark. Here I give one small detail and in the next paragraph a little more.

"He was a mountain of a man, black-haired, black-moustached, with a big nose and heavy jaw, like mine. His ears and nostrils sprouted black hairs as thick as wire but his eyes were babyish – like little brown velvet buttons. He had a low, slow voice and a laugh that shook the floorboards. I called him Poppo."

This description of Poppo, had it come before the reader had warmed to his generosity and kindliness, might have made a bad impression. I wanted to show him in a good light (he is, in fact, one of my favourite creations) but I also wanted to portray a mixture of roughness and gentleness. His low voice and loud laugh underline this aspect, and as the story develops he reveals a combination of weakness and strength in his nature.

In describing his appearance I also give the reader a clearer picture of Florence who has the same big nose and heavy jaw. Later I disclose that Florence also has warm brown eyes, like her father, but to have mentioned it in this paragraph would have overloaded the reader with impressions.

"I called him Poppo." This isolated sentence, coming, as it does, before a space dividing the chapter into sections, is meant to highlight the close and happy relationship between them. Nicknames, as I have said, are important to fiction; they are used in all manner of loving collaborations and for me it would be unthinkable to write a novel without them. Later in the book we learn that Poppo calls Florence "Janie"; he had wanted her to be christened Jane.

If you analyse for yourself the rest of the chapter, I think you will understand my reasons for introducing the various scenes and conversations. This kind of study, applied to any published novel of the sort you wish to write, can be extremely helpful.

14

The Title

"Eureka! I have found it!"
Archimedes

Some authors get the title before they begin the book. It comes like a bolt from heaven with no warning; two or three inspirational words are the starting signal for a marathon of eighty thousand. More often, however, the title has to come when the novel is completed.

How do you go about it?

First of all you might think about your theme, your setting, your central character and your peak situations. Make a list of all the key words that come to mind. Then juggle with them until you find the right combination. The title might express the theme: *Room at the Top*; *A Kind of Loving*; *The Cruel Sea*. Arresting titles often take the form of a paradox: *A Bouquet of Barbed Wire*; *The Crying Game*; *Bonjour Tristesse*; *A Raging Calm*; *A Fearful Joy*; *Casualties of Peace*.

The name of the protagonist may be suitable, either alone or with an additional word or two: *Lolita*; *Justine*; *Herzog*; *Billy Liar*; *Love for Lydia*. Or a place name: *Bhowani Junction*; *The House in Paris*; *Watership Down*; *The Purple Plain*.

A simple noun with only the definite article can be effective: *The Spire*; *The Collector*; *The Millstone*. Or a noun with one or more adjectives: *The Willow Cabin*; *The Black Prince*; *The Chinese Love Pavilion*; *The Country Girls*. Quotations are popular and you might discover one which suits your novel to perfection, but Shakespeare and the Bible have been rather overworked. You might find a colloquial phrase such as *"Ask me Tomorrow"*, *"Take a Girl Like You"*, *"I'm the King of the Castle"* and *"Three into Two Won't Go"* . . . . Finding a good title can be a long and difficult task but it is always fascinating. Study those you admire and analyse their relationship to the theme and the mood of the book. Don't be tempted into using a title which is artistic in itself but not really appropriate to your novel.

There is no copyright in titles, so you don't have legal worries, but it is unsatisfactory for you as well as for the other author if you stumble into a duplication. However, at this stage you only need a "working title". If your novel is accepted there will be plenty of time for you and your publisher to agree on the final choice.

15

Sending it off

"The book dies a real death for me when I write the last word. I have a little sorrow and then I go on to a new book which is alive."
John Steinbeck

A brief – very brief – preliminary letter to the publisher of your choice is always advisable. State the length and nature of your novel and ask if he is willing to consider it. Alternatively, you might decide to contact a literary agent.

It is important that your novel should be correctly and neatly typed. If it is a masterpiece it will probably be recognised as such in the end, no matter how badly it is presented, but with the fiction market as it is today it would be madness not to give your manuscript every possible advantage. Publishers are highly professional people and they like to think they are dealing with other professionals. Information on lay-out may be found in *The Writers' and Artists' Year Book*, *The Writer's Handbook* or *The Writer's Market*, but if you intend to prepare the final typescript yourself the following notes will be useful:

1) Use good quality typing paper (A4 in the UK/$8\frac{1}{2}''$ x 11'' in the USA) and take at least two carbon copies.
2) Use a black typewriter ribbon and be sure to replace it before it becomes faint.
3) Use double line-spacing on one side of the paper only and leave good margins, particularly on the left-hand side. See that each page has the same margins and the same number of lines.
4) Number the pages, either top or bottom.
5) Keep corrections to a minimum. If they cannot be avoided, make sure they are neatly printed in ink, using lower-case letters like typescript, not capitals.
6) In the centre of the first page give the title, with your name or pseudonym. Your name and address should appear at the top and be repeated on the last page, in case the title sheet comes adrift. At the bottom of the title page state the number of words, to the nearest thousand.
7) Fasten each chapter together separately with a paper clip and put the novel in a strong cardboard folder, or leave the pages loose in a typing-paper box.

8) Write a brief covering letter, stating merely that you are sending your first novel, entitled So-and-So for their consideration and enclosing stamps to cover return postage if unsuitable. If you want to be sure of an acknowledgement send a stamped, self-addressed postcard for the purpose. Some publishers, I'm afraid, are finding it necessary to cut down on these little courtesies.

9) Pack it carefully and send it by registered post or recorded delivery.

10) Be prepared to wait up to three months before hearing the verdict. During this period, do not write or telephone, and *on no account* call in person.

You might wonder how to decide which publisher to choose for the first attempt. Assuming that you are working without an agent, I suggest a visit to the public library to study the imprint of those novels you feel have most in common with yours. Consult your *Writers' and Artists' Year Book*, *Writer's Handbook*, etc. for addresses and requirements.

Don't be discouraged if it comes back – and comes back without comment. (It is not usual to give reasons.) We should never have had the chance to read *Gone with the Wind*, *Room at the Top*, *Catch 22*, *Watership Down* and many other famous novels if their authors – or agents – had not persisted in spite of early refusals. This book you are reading went to twenty-six publishers before it was accepted!

16

Writing for Teenagers

"Of all the compliments that can be paid to a writer, there is one especially that will make him glow with pleasure, namely: 'You are admired so much among the younger generation.' "
François Mauriac

The teenage novel is a form of writing which offers high rewards – in all senses of the word. There is a growing demand for this kind of book; many publishers are on the look-out for new authors who can fulfil the requirements.

In order to write well for this market I think you must love young people, respect them, communicate with them and understand their attitudes. The greatest dangers are to "talk down" and to moralise. Never preach – not even by inference – although of course, as in the adult novel, you will devise events which demonstrate certain truths. You will write most successfully for this age-group if these truths relate to the courage and good sense of young people. Ever since infancy, your readers will, from time to time, have been criticised, belittled, misunderstood and ignored by adults. Some will have been beaten and humiliated. When they begin to read novels for pleasure (and much of their previous reading will have been compulsory) they like to feel that the author – presumably an adult – is *on their side*. And so you must *be* on their side. It's no use pretending. Youngsters are experts in detecting hypocrisy, however immature they might be in other respects. Your adult characters should be shown as the fallible human beings they undoubtedly are. If the story is written with compassion it can do a great deal to bridge that painful "generation gap".

I think it would be unwise to attempt a novel of this kind if you disapprove of wild hair, tacky gear, loud pop music, etc. Obviously you don't have to like every aspect of the young scene but unless you look on it with affection and tolerance the teenage market is not for you.

The word "teenager" for the purpose of this chapter, means thirteen to sixteen, although the range of readers might sometimes include twelve- and seventeen-year-olds. "Young adult" is another term used in the publishing world. Novels for this age-group are mainly read by girls; teenage boys usually enjoy adult adventure stories such as *Jaws* and the James Bond sagas. It is therefore advisable to choose as your main character a girl of fifteen or sixteen. Her boy friend can be a little older. Try to make your background as "classless" as you can, so that a wide range of youngsters can identify with the heroine.

The length required varies between 25,000 and 35,000 words. These books are not illustrated and there are usually no titles to the chapters. In fact they are very much like straight adult novels except for the difference in length and in the age of the main character. There is also the question of pace. A teenage novel must *move*. There must be immediate action, a strong story, plenty of dialogue, and a steady development towards an unexpected climax. Most of the teenagers I have consulted prefer a happy ending, but their main requirement is a good *story*. They like short chapters and don't mind whether the novel is in the first person or not, so long as they can easily identify with the central character. They like the heroine to experience frustration, distress and danger but eventually to triumph through her own efforts – or the efforts of her boy friend. They want stories that deal with the kind of problems they have to face themselves, and there is no need to avoid unpleasant realities. Young people see the television news and read the papers. They know what goes on in the world and they need truth, not eye-wash. Gone are the days when all parents, teachers and policemen had to be shown in the best possible light. My own most successful novel for teenagers, *Escape on Monday*, concerns a girl who hates her mother. The mother deserves it, but I took pains to show that she is hateful on account of her own secret misery. When the girl realises this, she is able to come to terms with her situation.

Publishers vary a great deal in their attitudes to the various "taboos" – pre-marital sex, abortion, drug-addiction, racial prejudice, etc. – but I should say that almost any subject is acceptable *provided it is written in a sensitive and sympathetic manner*. It is my view that the treatment in fiction of a distressing problem, far from causing harm, can be helpful and comforting to those teenagers who are involved in a similar situation. For many of them, constantly meeting with hypocrisy and disapproval, the pages of a novel are a welcome source of honesty and understanding.

The characterisation should, of course, be as deeply felt and convincing as in an adult book. Descriptive passages should be short, but no less telling for that; atmosphere is vital. Write simply and directly in a lively style and avoid lengthy passages of introspection. Don't shy away from scenes of violent emotion, whether it be love, hatred, fear or jealousy. Your readers will be glad to know that they are not the only ones to harbour such feelings.

Try to establish good personal relationships with as many teenagers as possible. If there are none in your family, make an effort to meet them whenever you can and discuss their problems and interests. No matter what your age, young people are usually delighted to give their opinions on all subjects if they know you are a genuine friend. Watch television documentaries concerned with adolescents, read their magazines, listen in on their conversations in buses and shops. Go to pop concerts. Help at a youth club. Listen to a pop music station – you can learn a great deal from the disc jockeys. In many ways they have the attitude you need: they treat their young listeners as equals and are not ashamed to admit their own faults and weaknesses. This creates a sympathetic relationship because teenagers are usually insecure and nervous, no matter how brash they may appear on the surface. Read as many teenage novels as you can; your public library will tell you which are the most popular. Study the various styles and decide on your own approach.

What about slang? It must be used, of course, if the dialogue is to sound authentic, and you should make yourself familiar with the words that are in vogue. Any youngster will be glad to put you in the picture. Slang, together with clothes and popular songs, must be chosen for their staying power. The albums of Elton John, Bob Dylan and the Rolling Stones are likely to last for another decade at least. The same applies to the Beatles, in one form or another. There are many more to choose from and it's up to you to find them out. I've been lucky; I have introduced pop songs into my teenage novels for the past ten years and I can still find them all in the record shops.

In any case, it's a comfort to remember that you will have the opportunity of correcting the proofs of your book a few months before publication; you can bring it up to date at that stage, provided your alterations are minimal.

Make sure that your novel has the ring of truth. Youngsters think deeply, feel deeply, and care about social issues. They respect honesty. They love fun. They are also selfish, arrogant and lazy –

just as we were at their age. Most of them love to hear an absorbing tale, but many have yet to form the habit of reading for pleasure. If your story can beguile them into curling up with a book, you have done them a service for life.

Writing for young people is a great challenge. Lasting impressions are received at that age, characters and events can stick in the memory and mould their thinking. Don't sermonise, whatever you do, but be aware of your opportunity to tell a rattling good story and also to leave your readers with something of value to think about.

17

Agents, Publishers and Reviewers

"If a publisher declines your manuscript, remember it is merely the
decision of one fallible human being, and try another."
Sir Stanley Unwin

Agents and Publishers

I think a novelist is well advised to employ a literary agent.
There may be paperback rights to negotiate, not to mention foreign
rights, broadcasting and television rights, serial rights, etc. If you
have no agent, the publisher will expect to handle these matters on
your behalf. You might be content with this, but sometimes an
agent can obtain better terms for you. Naturally enough, no agent
is willing to take on a book unless he thinks it saleable, so you
should send return postage in the first instance. Choose one from
The Writers' and Artists' Year Book, *The Writer's Handbook*, etc.
and ask for the latest information on his terms before you send the
book. Remember no reputable agent demands payment of any kind
until he has found you a publisher.

Once an agent has agreed to handle your book you can sit back
and let him do all the work – choosing suitable publishers, sending
it out, paying postage, etc. If you don't hear from him you will
know that he has not received an offer of publication so don't
badger him. Where agents are concerned, no news is nearly always
bad news! If he sells your book, he will deduct his 10% commission
from the monies due to you, so you will never have to pay anything
directly out of your own pocket. A friendly agent is always glad to
advise you on any matter in connection with your work and most
novelists find it comforting to have someone to do any necessary
wrangling about contracts and royalties while they concentrate on
writing the next book. For the vague, dreamy kind of writer with
no business sense, an agent is essential.

Agents and publishers often spend a lot of time together over
leisurely luncheons and get to know each other very well. This is in
our interest, of course, but it is bound to lead to a kind of
camaraderie from which the novelist, possibly up in town for the
day from some rural hide-out, is bound to feel somewhat excluded.
I think it is part of the policy to make authors feel unimportant and

even a little in the way! This is possibly a clever manoeuvre to counteract our natural egotism, so we must take it in our stride and try to see the set-up from their angle as well.

I think it is a fallacy that publishers take more notice of a novel received from an agent. Initially perhaps, but provided the manuscript is presented in a professional manner, they will look at it, as they look at all new novels, in the profound hope that a masterpiece has dropped into their laps. Every typescript is carefully assessed before it is returned. This does not mean, of course, that the book is necessarily read right through; the first few pages can often prove beyond doubt that the writer lacks the skill to produce a saleable novel. But no publisher is going to risk letting a best-seller slip through his fingers if he can help it.

Before you have found one who is willing to publish your novel, publishers seem like a race apart, a godlike, omnipotent breed with the power to cast you into hell or grant you everlasting bliss. Bliss it certainly is, when it happens, and let no cynic persuade you otherwise, but it is not everlasting. Wait until you see what percentage you receive of your paperback earnings!

Once the contract is signed, you are dependent on your publisher to print, publicise and sell your book as he thinks fit. He is an expert – or should be – and uninformed suggestions are not likely to be welcomed. But it's *your book*. You have slaved over it for months or even years, and you are emotionally involved with it in much the same way as a mother is involved in the affairs of her child. Nevertheless, your book-child is taken from you into this vast foster-home, given a jacket that you possibly hate, and launched on the nation with a degree and manner of publicity that you might or might not agree with. The whole affair is out of your hands and nobody seems to understand – or care – how helpless you feel. All your publisher really wants from you now is another novel, better than the last. And another. . . . This is quite reasonable; he is taking a big chance. First novels don't usually earn very much for anybody, at least not in the hard-cover edition. You're jolly lucky if you sell 3,000 copies. You couldn't do without him and you are fortunate to have found someone who is willing to launch you. On the other hand, he couldn't do without his authors, and we sometimes feel that publishers, like agents, don't fully appreciate our indispensability.

If your novel is accepted, the publisher might suggest certain minor alterations. Pay great attention to these suggestions. If you adopt them, you will probably improve your book considerably.

Nevertheless, stand firm if you strongly disagree; he will usually respect your wishes unless he sees himself in court on a charge of libel or obscenity.

Finally, here are a few Don'ts:

1) Don't ever consider paying for publication of your novel; if it is up to standard you will eventually find a publisher who will offer you a proper contract.

2) Don't telephone or visit your publisher without a genuine reason.

3) Don't telephone if a letter will do just as well, and keep your letters brief and strictly to the point.

4) Don't mention personal problems unless it is absolutely essential.

5) Don't promise a date for delivery of a manuscript unless you are sure you can honour it. Establish a reputation for reliability and efficiency.

6) Don't make too many alterations on your proof copy when it is sent to you for checking. These are costly. Be sure the book is right as far as possible before it goes to the printers.

7) If you have a justifiable complaint, don't hesitate to mention it simply for fear of being unpopular.

8) Don't forget that the author-publisher relationship is inclined to be a delicate one. If you are angry, sleep on it and calm down before writing or telephoning.

Reviewers

If you publish a novel you lay yourself open to every reviewer's opinion and you must accept his right to express it forcibly and publicly. Remember it is only one person's view and you cannot hope to please everyone. Consider every adverse comment with care and learn from it what you can. Never write up and argue with a reviewer unless he has made a grave error on some point of *fact*.

It was not until my own first novel was published that I realised just how diverse the views of the critics can be. Instead of reading, at the most, four or five reviews of the same book, I found myself reading fifty. The following quotations from some of them will amuse you and illustrate my point:

"The ending is rather flat." (*Washington Sunday Star*)
"The nerve racking climax is well managed." (*Books of the Month*)

"Has no virtues to distinguish it from countless others." (*Surrey Comet*)

"The outstanding first novel from the Spring publishing lists." (*Books and Bookmen*)

"Shivery and generally unpleasant." (*Saturday Review*)

"An endearing and charming novel." (*New York Morning Telegraph*)

"A lurid pot-pourri of base motives." (*Washington Post*)

"A novel of warmth and understanding." (*New York Times*)

"Intricate story." (*Kentish Observer*)

"The story is simple enough." (*Surrey Comet*)

"Shaky on credibility." (*Yorkshire Post*)

"Convincing." (*Evening Standard*)

"The book was a struggle to read." (*Seattle Post*)

"Highly readable first novel of unusually high calibre." (*Smith's Trade News*)

So why worry?

18

Payment and Contracts

"I simply don't know how anyone can write at great speed, and only for the money's sake."

Feodor Dostoevsky

Payment

The story of payment for novels is not a happy one. Unless you reach the best-seller class, your success is badly rewarded compared with most other professions. Nevertheless, there is always the possibility of big money round the corner. Any post could bring news of a sale that might mean hundreds – or even thousands – of pounds. And there's always the hope that the next book you write will really hit the high spots.

I have been comparatively lucky; all my novels have been published as paperbacks, I've had good foreign sales, and sold three film options (although the pictures were never made). However, it takes me two years to write a novel, and my average income has never been very high.

I would advise any new novelist who must earn a living, to take another job as well – at least part time. It is bad for one's work to write for money with a sense of urgency and anxiety, although a certain degree of incentive and a self-imposed deadline can be beneficial. It is advisable to choose a bread-winning job which entails meeting people, travelling, getting out of doors. As soon as you make a satisfactory income as a novelist you can give up the other occupation and write full time.

The Contract

Under no circumstances should you agree to an outright sale of the copyright of your novel. Few publishers today would expect it.

The contract is an agreement form printed by the publisher or agent, with blanks for the insertion of the title and author, royalty rates, the sum payable in advance, etc. Study it very carefully and ask for an explanation of any clause which is not clear to you. If you belong to the Society of Authors (84 Drayton Gardens, London SW10) or the Writer's Guild of Great Britain (430 Edgware Road, London W2) or in America to the Authors'

Guild/Authors' League (234 West 44th Street, New York, NY 10036) they will check your contract before you sign it and give you any other advice you may need. I strongly recommend every published writer to join one of these organisations; there are a great many advantages.

The following contract for one of my teenage novels will give you an idea of the kind of agreement you would receive if you employed an agent. For an adult novel on both sides of the Atlantic the traditional starting royalty is 10 per cent.

Memorandum of Agreement made this 4ᵗ day of May 1973

BETWEEN **Mrs. DIANNE DOUBTFIRE c/o Curtis Brown Limited of 1 Craven Hill, London, W2 3BW**

(hereinafter called the PROPRIETOR) of the one part AND Messrs. ▮▮▮▮▮▮▮▮▮▮

(hereinafter called the PUBLISHERS) of the other part WHEREBY it is mutually agreed as follows concerning a work at present entitled:

▮▮▮▮▮▮▮▮▮▮

by **Dianne Doubtfire**

1. The PUBLISHERS, subject to the conditions following, shall during the legal term of copyright have a licence to produce and publish and sell the said work in volume form in the English language. This licence shall be an exclusive licence throughout the British Commonwealth and Empire as politically constituted at the date of this agreement ‒ ‒ ‒ ‒ ‒ ‒ ‒ ‒ ‒ ‒ ‒ ‒ ‒ ‒ ‒ ‒ but including the Republic of South Africa, the Irish Republic, Burma, Egypt, Iraq,/Pakistan, Bangla Israel, Jordan and the British Trusteeships. The licence shall be non-exclusive through-/desh out the rest of the world except ‒ ‒ ‒ ‒ ‒ ‒ ‒ ‒ ‒ , the United States of America, its Colonies and Dependencies and the Philippine Islands.

Territory

2. The PUBLISHERS shall unless prevented by circumstances beyond their control publish the said work within one year from the date of delivery to them of the completed manuscript ready for press. The published price shall be about net in the first instance. All details as to the manner of production publication and the number and destination of free copies shall be left to the sole discretion of the PUBLISHERS who shall bear all expenses in connection therewith except the amount (if any) of Author's corrections in the proofs other than printers' errors in excess of 15% (fifteen per 10% (ten per cent) of the cost of composition. The PUBLISHERS shall notify the PROPRIETOR cent) of any such excess expenses and the extra amount shall be borne by the PROPRIETOR and settled in account. The PUBLISHERS shall on completion of printing and production use their best endeavours to return direct to the PROPRIETOR his typescript (s), on request.

Publication

3. The PUBLISHERS agree to print the following words on the reverse of the title page:

Copyright Notice

© Dianne Doubtfire 197*
(*This indicates the actual year of publication)

4. The PUBLISHERS shall send to the PROPRIETOR or his representatives on the day of first publication seven presentation copies of the said work and the PROPRIETOR shall be entitled to purchase further copies for personal use at the lowest trade price.

Presentation Copies

Initialled by: ▮▮ DD

73

5. The manuscript, which shall be approximately **25,000** words in length, shall be delivered by ~~30th June~~ 31st August 1973 The PROPRIETOR shall, at his own expense, supply the PUBLISHERS with an index, if requested.

Delivery of Manuscript and Index

6. ~~The PROPRIETOR shall supply at his own expense/at the expense of the~~ PUBLISHERS all photographs pictures diagrams ~~maps and/or~~ other illustrations for the said work. In respect ~~of any photographs~~ etc. or any copyright material, he shall obtain ~~from the~~ owners of the respective copyrights written permission to ~~reproduce such material in connection with the said work.~~

Illustrations

7. Accounts of the sales of the said work shall be made up to the **31st** day of **December** in each year and delivered and settled within **three** months thereafter. The PUBLISHERS shall in the first two years following publication make up half-yearly statements of sales to the **30th** day of **June** and deliver and settle these within **three** months thereafter. The PUBLISHERS shall pay the PROPRIETOR as follows:

Accounts and Royalties

(a) On copies of the full-priced editions sold in the Home Market:

Full-Priced Home

A royalty of 7½% (seven and one-half percent) of the published price on all copies sold up to 4,000 (four thousand); and 10% (ten percent) on all copies sold thereafter.

(b) On Cheaper editions issued by the PUBLISHERS and sold in the Home Market:

Cheap Home

A royalty of 10% of the published price on copies sold of any editions issued at or below one-half of the original published price,

(c) On copies of the full-priced editions sold at special discount of 45% or more Overseas and in Great Britain for the purpose of export: A royalty ~~on the original English published price of:£~~ on the price received of:

Full-Priced Export

10% (ten percent) on all copies sold.

(d) On copies of Cheaper editions sold at special discount of 45% or more Overseas and in Great Britain for the purpose of export:

Cheap Export

A royalty of 10% of the price received on copies sold of editions issued at or below one-half of the original published price.

(e) A royalty to be mutually agreed on sales of any Australian edition published in Australasia, either under the PUBLISHERS' own imprint or by arrangement with another publisher.

Australasia

Initialled by:

74

(f)   10% (Ten per cent.) of the sum received from the sale of any copies of the said work as a remainder unless such copies shall be sold at or below cost when no royalty shall be paid to the PROPRIETOR. The PROPRIETOR shall be given the option for fourteen days of purchasing such copies at the remainder price.   *Remainders*

(g)   (i)   Should the PUBLISHERS, with the consent of the PROPRIETOR, sub-lease any part of this licence to a reprint book club or for condensation in volume form, then provided that the original Publisher does not manufacture the book or arrange to participate with the sub-lessee on each individual book in any way, any gross sums received from the sub-lease shall be divided   50%   to the PROPRIETOR and   50%   to the PUBLISHERS.   *Sub-leases*

(ii)   Should the PUBLISHERS, with the consent of the PROPRIETOR, sub-lease any part of this licence to a cheap edition publisher then, provided that the original publisher does not manufacture the book or arrange to participate with the sub-lessee on each individual book in any way, any gross sums received from the sub-lease shall be divided:

50% to the PROPRIETOR if royalty is $7\frac{1}{2}$%;
55% to the PROPRIETOR if royalty is 10%; and
60% to the PROPRIETOR if royalty is $12\frac{1}{2}$%.

(iii)   Should the PUBLISHERS, with the consent of the PROPRIETOR, arrange that a Book Club or similar organization take sheets or bound copies manufactured in whole or in part by the PUBLISHERS, the royalty payable to the PROPRIETOR shall be mutually agreed.

(iv)   The PUBLISHERS shall pay to the PROPRIETOR all advances due under clauses (g) (i) and (ii) within one month of receipt by them, **provided that the original advance has been earned.**

(h)   Any gross sums received by the PUBLISHERS from the granting of permissions to any American publisher or Book Club to distribute in territory exclusively granted to the English publisher shall be divided equally between the PROPRIETOR and the PUBLISHERS.   *American Entry*

(i)   The PUBLISHERS shall have the sole right to sub-lease anthology and quotation rights and shall pay to the PROPRIETOR 50% (Fifty per cent.) of the gross receipts.   *Anthology*

(j)   The PUBLISHERS shall be entitled to authorise free of charge the recording of the work in Braille or as a Talking Book for the use of the blind and/or the microfilming of the work for the use of handicapped persons, such permissions to be given only for use of the material on a non-commercial basis.   *Braille etc.*

(k)   No royalties shall be paid on copies given away in the interests of the said work.   *Free Copies*

(l)   Advance Payment
A sum on account of the afore-mentioned monies, but not returnable, of   *Advance*
£150 (One hundred and fifty pounds) payable half on signature of this agreement by both parties and half on day of publication of the said work.

Initialled by:  *DO*

8. It is agreed that the PUBLISHERS shall receive the following shares of the net monies received by the PROPRIETOR from any sale or lease of the following rights made during the validity of this agreement and in the territory exclusively granted under it:

(a) The right to publish the book or excerpts from it or illustrations based on it in two or more instalments of a periodical if such rights are sold after book publication: 25% (Twenty-five per cent.)

(b) The right to publish the book in whole or in a condensed form in a single issue of a periodical: 25% **if such rights are sold before book publication** and 50% **if such rights are sold after book publication.**

(c) The right to read the book or excerpts from it over the radio or over television, either as a single item or serially: 25% (Twenty-five per cent.) The PUBLISHERS shall receive no share in any monies received from the writing for radio or television of a play based on the book either for performances as a whole or in instalments.

(d) The right to produce or reproduce the work or any part thereof by film micrography, xerography or by gramophone records or by the means of any other contrivance whether by sight or sound or a combination of both: 25% (Twenty-five per cent.)

9. The PUBLISHERS, who have no interest in or control of film rights, agree that after publication under this Agreement, a film company shall have an unencumbered right to print and publish for use only in advertising the film, synopses (including quotations) of not more than ~~10,000~~ 5,000 words in the territory above specified.

10. If the PUBLISHERS give notice at any time that in their opinion the demand for the said work has ceased or if less than twelve copies are shown to have been sold in any six months' statement or if less than 50 copies remain in stock and the PUBLISHERS fail thereafter to issue a new edition within six months of having received written notice from the PROPRIETOR or his representatives, then this agreement shall automatically determine without prejudice to any claim which the PROPRIETOR may have either for monies due and/or damages and/or otherwise. If the PUBLISHERS go into liquidation, other than voluntary liquidation for the purpose of reconstruction, or if payment should not be made by the PUBLISHERS of monies due or statements delivered to the PROPRIETOR as agreed herein within three months after date of a written demand from the PROPRIETOR or his representatives for such payment or such delivery then in either of these cases this agreement shall automatically determine without prejudice to any claim which the PROPRIETOR may have either for monies and/or damages and/or otherwise.

Initialled by:

11.   The PROPRIETOR hereby warrants to the PUBLISHERS that the said [Libel] work is in no way whatsoever an infringement of any existing copyright and that it contains nothing obscene or which with the intention of the PROPRIETOR is libellous, and the PROPRIETOR will indemnify the PUBLISHERS against any loss, injury or damage (including any legal costs or expenses properly incurred) occasioned to the PUBLISHERS in consequence of any breach (unknown to the PUBLISHERS) of this warranty.

12.   This agreement shall not be construed as granting or conveying to the PUBLISHERS any rights or interests other than those which are specifically set forth herein.

13.   All monies due under this agreement shall be paid to the PROPRIETOR'S representatives, Curtis Brown Limited of 1 Craven Hill, London W2 3EW, whose receipt shall be a discharge of the monies received and the said Curtis Brown Limited is hereby empowered by the PROPRIETOR to conduct negotiations with the PUBLISHERS in respect of all matters arising in any way out of this agreement.

Publishers .... Chairman

Managing Director

Proprietor ....

19

The Need for Integrity

"We simply paint humanity as we find it, as it is. We say let all be made known in order that all may be healed."
Emile Zola

There are no easy conclusions about the ethics of novel-writing, but I will give you my carefully considered opinion, if only as a basis for discussion.

Let's admit, first of all, that our society is a vast fabric of deceits and superficialities and that too many of us are afraid of revealing – or even perhaps of *knowing* – the truth about ourselves. How often do we try to make out that we're cleverer, richer, younger, kinder, more industrious or successful than we really are? (Or poorer, sicker and unluckier – it's all part of the same story.) It seems to me that the only faces with nothing to hide are looking out of prams!

This transparent shell under which we try to conceal our genuine selves is, of course, a menace to happy personal relationships, but what concerns us here is its effect on the novels we write.

The serious novelist must abandon all false and phoney attitudes. He must analyse his own motives, assess his own weaknesses, uncover his secret fears and pains without shame; only in this way can he achieve the self-knowledge he needs as a basis for understanding others and for creating full-blooded characters and convincing situations. If he is to develop as a writer he must be prepared to look at every aspect of life with the clean eye that sees without judging. "This," he will say, "whether we like it or not, is the way people *are*; let's try to get inside their minds and understand what makes them behave as they do." Your task as a novelist is to strip off veneers and lay bare the essential pith of people, places and things, revealing as best you can their true nature and their relationship with each other.

Many readers shrink from looking at the essence of things because it brings them up against a reality they wish to evade. Such people want to stay on the surface of life; a novel might plunge them down too deeply. And yet, paradoxically, those very depths can offer the heights of freedom and release we all secretly long for.

You may have pondered on the reason why a novel or play with a tragic theme can, if beautifully written, have a strangely uplifting effect. Could it be because one has achieved, through involvement, a larger understanding and a greater maturity of vision?

When the ethics of the novel are discussed, the main problem seems to be sex. People are often embarrassed or disgusted by "earthy" writing for a variety of reasons – upbringing, religion, personal unhappiness – but no matter what his attitude may be, the writer must accept the fact that sexual love has been the mainspring of fiction throughout the ages. It drives men and women to the limits of joy and despair; this is the stuff of drama. Of course there are many novels of great quality which make little or no reference to sex, and every novelist chooses his theme to suit his own approach.

I think it is a grave mistake to allow oneself to be inhibited by thoughts of what friends and relations might say if the book were to be published. This kind of restraint is death to good fiction. *"My favourite novelists,"* says Alberto Moravia, *"are the ones who empty out their bag and say everything they have to say right to the end without regard for the conformisms of their own or future times."* And again: *"The writer who practises compromise lacks the courage to get to the bottom of things while knowing full well in his heart that this bottom exists; that is, he does not dare to be* extreme. *He preserves a conventional golden mean, like someone who avoids saying what he thinks at a polite reception for fear of not being asked again."*

To put sex into a novel for commercial gain is totally wrong, but surely it is also wrong to leave it out for fear of shocking the puritans? A writer of integrity cannot allow himself to be hampered by the possible disapproval of a certain section of the reading public. Is he to keep saying to himself as he writes: "Oh, dear, no – I can't put *that*! What would Aunt Mabel say?" He is not writing the book for Aunt Mabel. He is writing, let us hope, because he is profoundly moved by ideas which cry out for expression. The only kind of censorship I would advocate is that which the writer himself imposes upon his work. Each has his own taboos; they are an essential part of his individuality. For me, war and sadism are the great obscenities but so long as they are exposed for what they are, this does not mean that I cannot include them in my books. Cruelty, as well as tenderness, is a part of life; fear as well as faith, lust as well as love . . . a balance must be maintained if we are to portray reality.

79

A good novel can break down a great many barriers by uncovering the secret feelings that are common to all mankind but seldom communicated. In a novel you can say the things that are too intimate and too important to talk about – even to your dearest friend. This is not only a release for the novelist but also for those readers of like nature who enjoy his books. No one is compelled to read a novel he dislikes. The reader is free; the writer must also be free. He must create his book as a complete and individual work of art, with nothing added and nothing omitted to distort the perfect shape as he sees it.

20

The Creative Mood

"To live in the world of creation – to get into it and stay in it – to frequent it and haunt it – to think intensely and fruitfully – to woo combinations and inspirations into being by a depth and continuity of attention and meditation – this is the only thing."
Henry James

No amount of talent and craftsmanship can be of much avail without the creative mood, but with all three working together you could create a novel to rock the nations!

How, then, do we capture this elusive but vital ingredient? Talent is a gift we are born with, technique can be learned, but the creative mood is here one minute and gone the next. It can be snatched away from us by a telephone call, a broken fingernail or even a fleeting thought.

Of course, we cannot always be in the mood and we must sit down to write however little we "feel like it". Writing a novel is a hard job of work and you can make some very useful progress without being in a frenzy of inspiration. Train yourself – quite gently – not to be a slave to your moods. The majority of successful writers treat their work like an office job; they might keep unusual hours but there is a pattern of regularity in their stints. If you can get into the habit of regular work, however little time you can manage at first, I think you will find that the creative mood develops as you become involved in the current chapter.

Sometimes, of course, it just doesn't happen. No matter how hard you try, there are no words, no new ideas. On these occasions you will have to devise a way of coaxing yourself back into action. For me it might be a walk, a chat with a sympathetic friend, a hot bath or a Scotch and soda, but what helps me most of all is to read a few comments on writing by well-loved authors. Depression can be a dangerous enemy if I don't catch it in time; it can drag me down into apathy and even prevent me from going to the bookcase to find the quotations which could restore my balance. If, however, I force myself to make the effort, those extracts can move me to pick up my pencil again with that tingle of excitement which we all know so well and need so desperately.

Here are some examples, taken at random, as they are when I

use them to recapture my writing mood.

I love my work with a frenzied perverted passion, as an ascetic loves the hair-shirt that scrapes his body. Sometimes, when I find myself empty, when expression won't come, when, after scribbling long pages, I find I haven't written a sentence, then I fall on the couch and lie there, stupefied in an inward slough of despond.

I hate myself, and blame myself, for this frenzy of pride which makes me pant for mere imaginings. A quarter of an hour later, everything has altered; my heart is pounding for joy. Last Wednesday I had to get up to find my handkerchief: tears were running down my face. I had moved myself to tears in writing, revelling deliciously in the emotions of my own conception, in the sentence which rendered it, and in the pleasure of having found it.

Gustave Flaubert

My first thought about art, as a child, was that the artist brings something into the world that didn't exist before, and that he does it without destroying something else. . . . That still seems to me its central magic, its core of joy.

John Updike

I hear . . . that you are having trouble writing. God! I know this feeling so well. I think it is never coming back – but it does – one morning, there it is again.

About a year ago, Bob Anderson (the playwright) asked me for help in the same problem. I told him to write poetry – not for selling – not even for seeing – poetry to throw away. For poetry is the mathematics of writing and closely kin to music. And it is also the best therapy because sometimes the troubles come tumbling out.

Well, he did . . . and I have three joyous letters from him saying it worked. Just poetry – anything and not designed for a reader. It's a great and valuable privacy.

I only offer this if your dryness goes on too long and makes you too miserable. You may come out of it any day. I have. The words are fighting each other to get out.

John Steinbeck

Always dream and shoot higher than you know you can do . . . Try to be better than yourself.

William Faulkner

To be truly happy is a question of how we begin and not of how we end, of what we want and not of what we have.

Robert Louis Stevenson

". . . The proper stuff of fiction" does not exist; everything is the proper stuff of fiction, every feeling, every thought; every quality of brain and spirit is drawn upon; no perception comes amiss. And if we can imagine the art of fiction come alive and standing in our midst, she would undoubtedly bid us break her and bully her, as well as honour and love her, for so her youth is renewed and her sovereignty assured.

Virginia Woolf

All those who live as literary men, – working daily as literary labourers, – will agree with me that three hours a day will produce as much as a man ought to write. But then, he should so have trained himself that he shall be able to work continuously during those three hours, – so have tutored his mind that it shall not be necessary for him to sit nibbling his pen, and gazing at the wall before him, till he shall have found the words with which he wants to express his ideas.

Anthony Trollope

The creative mood has a lot to do with confidence, and an understanding of the problems of the great can help us to put our own into perspective and not to worry unduly about them.

For me there is a perilous gap between the ideal I have in mind when I first envisage a novel, and the book that is at last completed. What can we do to bring the book we actually write into line with the book we believe, in moments of sublime self-assurance, that we are capable of writing? How can we preserve for months – or even years – the freshness of that first inspiration and develop it steadily into a satisfying whole? How do we avoid the doubts, the disintegration, the dying of the spark?

It is, of course, impossible to close the gap entirely. It may not even be desirable to do so: the constant struggle towards an elusive goal is a fine stimulus. Nevertheless, I think most of us would be glad to narrow the gulf a good deal further.

If the failure were due to lack of talent or technique there would be little more to say: without these one would hardly expect to succeed. But there is something else, and I believe that the root of the trouble may lie in the onset of anxiety. Anxiety can kill the creative mood and it often arises when the initial excitement dies away and the actual work begins. Those first ravishing concepts must be translated into a weighty pile of typescript if they are to be communicated. They must be retained and expanded, and this is one of the most daunting problems a novelist has to overcome.

It is a well-known fact that every impression is safely preserved in some mysterious storehouse of the mind; text-book knowledge we acquired as children can be charmed out of us under hypnosis. Surely, then, ideas quite recently conceived can't possibly be lost beyond recall. They will return, as a forgotten name returns, unless we drive them away by trying too hard to remember them. In the same way, that elusive mood of confidence and creativity will also return. I agree with Albert Camus when he says in his *Carnets: "A writer should not talk about his doubts about his creation. It would be too easy to reply to him: 'Who forces you to create? If it is so continuous an anguish, why do you bear it?' Our doubts are the most personal thing we have. Never speak of one's doubts – whatever they may be."*

In recent months I have been making a practical experiment which has amazed and delighted me. I find that it is possible, with practice, to surrender my apprehensions for short periods by a conscious effort of "letting-go", rather as one might cheerfully say, when a name eludes one, "Never mind, it'll come," instead of fretting about it. I relax in an easy chair for ten minutes or so before starting work and try to relinquish my anxieties. A deliberate slackening of muscular tension calms the mind and, conversely, the body becomes more relaxed when the mind is untroubled. After many abortive efforts I was able to let go, both mentally and physically. The effect on my writing was remarkable. Blockages were removed and long-standing problems were resolved as if by magic. The creative impulse was free to express itself.

Having proved the value of this approach, my confidence grew. Mental energy once wasted on worry was directed towards constructive work. My only regret is that I didn't tumble to it years ago.

It is impossible to write your best unless your mind is focused entirely on the task in hand. Personal anxieties beset us all, but we must nevertheless develop that "depth and continuity of attention and meditation" if we are to succeed as novelists. It can never be easy, but worth-while attainments seldom are. I'd like to leave you with another quotation from Robert Louis Stevenson: *"If any man love the labour of any trade . . . the gods have called him."*

Bibliography

Walter Allen (ed.): **Writers on Writing**, Phoenix House, London, and E. P. Dutton, New York

Miriam Allott: **Novelists on the Novel**, Routledge and Kegan Paul, London and Boston, MA

Geoffrey Ashe: **The Art of Writing Made Simple**, William Heinemann, London, and Doubleday & Co. Inc., New York

Theodore M. Bernstein: **The Careful Writer**, Atheneum, New York

Anthony Blond: **The Publishing Game**, Jonathan Cape, London

Malcolm Bradbury (ed.): **The Novel Today**, Fontana/Collins, London, and Rowman & Littlefield, Totowa, New Jersey

John Braine: **Writing a Novel**, Eyre Methuen, London, and McGraw-Hill Book Co., New York

Albert Camus: **Carnets** (2 volumes), Hamish Hamilton, London, and as **Notebooks 1942–1951**, Alfred A. Knopf, New York

R. V. Cassill: **Writing Fiction**, Prentice Hall, New Jersey

Christopher Derrick: **Reader's Report**, Victor Gollancz, London

E. M. Forster: **Aspects of the Novel**, Edward Arnold, London, and Harcourt, Brace, Jovanovich, New York

Pamela Frankau: **Pen to Paper**, William Heinemann, London

Michael Howard: **Jonathan Cape, Publisher**, Jonathan Cape, London

Victor Jones: **Teach Yourself Creative Writing**, St Paul's House, London

Michael Legat: **Dear Author**, Pelham Books, London

R. W. B. Lewis: **The Picaresque Saint**, Victor Gollancz, London

Somerset Maugham: **A Writer's Handbook**, William Heinemann, London, and Arno Press, New York

André Maurois: **The Art of Writing**, Bodley Head, London, and Arno Press, New York

Alberto Moravia: **Man as an End**, Secker & Warburg, London, and Farrar, Straus and Giroux Inc., New York

Paris Review Interviews: **Writers at Work** (4 volumes), Secker and Warburg, London, and Viking Press Inc., New York

V. S. Pritchett: **The Working Novelist**, Chatto and Windus, London

Frederic Raphael (ed.): **Bookmarks**, Jonathan Cape, London

Alain Robbe-Grillet: **Towards a New Novel**, John Calder, London, and Grove Press Inc., New York

John Steinbeck: **Journal of a Novel**, William Heinemann, London, and Viking Press Inc., New York

Stanley Unwin: **The Truth About Publishing**, Allen and Unwin, London and Winchester, MA

Angus Wilson: **The Wild Garden**, Secker and Warburg, London, and University of California Press, Berkeley, CA

Index of Authors Quoted